IMAGES
of America

THE HOMEWOOD
CEMETERY

ON THE COVER: Several water features, such as this one, have dotted the landscape of The Homewood Cemetery from its inception through the current day. This particular pond was filled in during the middle of the 20th century. Although not all of the original lakes and ponds have survived, many guests still visit the natural spring–fed pool inside the main gates. (Courtesy of The Homewood Cemetery.)

IMAGES
of America

THE HOMEWOOD
CEMETERY

Lisa Speranza

ARCADIA
PUBLISHING

Published by Arcadia Publishing
Charleston, South Carolina

Printed in the United States of America

Library of Congress Control Number: 2019944374

For all general information, please contact Arcadia Publishing:
Telephone 843-853-2070
Fax 843-853-0044
E-mail sales@arcadiapublishing.com
For customer service and orders:
Toll-Free 1-888-313-2665

Visit us on the Internet at www.arcadiapublishing.com

Dedicated to the lives and the legacies of the individuals within this book and the thousands of others at rest within The Homewood Cemetery.

"Think not that my life has been futile, nor grieve for an unsaid word, for all that my lips might never sing, my singing heart has heard." —Francis Fowler Hogan

CONTENTS

ACKNOWLEDGMENTS

To my light—my beloved daughter, Becca—may this serve to remind you, as you journey forward, to always follow your heart and pursue adventures you hold dear. The challenges will be numerous but worthwhile, and with your courage, dedication, and perseverance, you will surely achieve your dreams.

To my parents, I extend my most humble and sincere appreciation for your understanding, patience, and constant encouragement. Nothing I do in life would be possible without these, and I am ever grateful for them and you.

To my treasured friends Nancy, Roger, and Deb, I find myself in awe of your storytelling, kindness, and perpetually uplifting thoughtfulness. I additionally offer my gratitude to The Homewood Cemetery, including Pres. David Michener, Supt. Mike Joyce, Marilyn Evert, Janet Kettering, and numerous grounds and support staff.

I wish to recognize, with gratitude and admiration, the leadership of William Duff McCrady, longtime chairman of The Homewood Cemetery, and Edward W. Seifert of The Homewood Cemetery Historical Fund. It is due to their devotion and guidance over the last several decades—and the stewardship of Mary M. Unkovic, chairwoman of the historical fund—that The Homewood Cemetery remains a historic treasure and in much the same state as when these photographs were taken.

To those who entrusted me with your memories, legacies, photographs, and stories, I offer my utmost respect and appreciation. To Walter Rutkowski, Eric Zahren, Jewels Phraner, and the staff of the Carnegie Hero Fund Commission; Patti Benaglio and the staff of Hartwood Acres; Gez Ebbert; Elizabeth Burgwin; Dr. Ellsworth and Joanne Bowser; and Jamie Edwards—none of this would have been possible without each of you, and your contribution to this collection is as essential as my own.

Furthermore, I wish to thank the East End community as a whole. During the time this book was being written, the community was touched by unspeakable tragedy, and its response personified values it has always held dear—faith, strength, family, love, and courage. I hope to capture even the smallest portion of that. Lastly, thank you, dear reader, for sharing in this journey.

INTRODUCTION

From the very beginning, the grounds now occupied by The Homewood Cemetery have been a place of respite. Centuries ago, these rolling hills were covered by a rich forest, the trees of which would have provided cooling shade when the searing winds of summer scorched the region. In the late 1700s, this once sparsely populated area began to develop. The first residence in the area, Summerset, was built by Col. James Burd in 1760. Others soon followed, such as Ambrose Newton's estate and John Turner's abode, Federal Hill. In the midst of these grand estates, a small Russian cottage sat alone on a hill; it is the first known residence on the grounds that would later become The Homewood Cemetery.

At the beginning of the 19th century, the nearby city of Pittsburgh was on the cusp of transforming into a burgeoning industrialized giant. Many influential Pittsburgh families continued to establish residences in the serene landscape of the East End. Among them was the family of Judge William Wilkins. In the early 1830s, construction began on the family's estate, called Homewood. It was a vast manor atop the sprawling hills and amidst the sylvan woodlands that had graced the area for centuries. The home sat far enough away from the developing city to provide a sanctuary but also was close enough to allow William Wilkins to participate in cultivating the changes that were occurring in the city at that time.

As Pittsburgh became less known for being a sleepy gateway to the west and more as a progressive force in areas such as politics and industry, several notable names began to arise. This trend would continue, and by the mid- to late 19th century, many well-known Pittsburgh families called the East End home.

In 1865, Judge William Wilkins died. Like many members of prominent families, he was buried in nearby Allegheny Cemetery, which was the best-known burial ground in the city at that time. When it opened in 1844, it was designed as a rural cemetery, featuring winding paths, ornate monuments and fencing, and many hallmarks that further enhanced its garden-like design.

After the death of William Wilkins, Homewood was put up for sale. Recognizing the need for a second large burial ground in the area, 178 acres of Wilkins's former estate was purchased with the intention of developing it into a large cemetery for Pittsburgh's East End residents. The area had become a haven for numerous wealthy families, and the need for a burying ground located closer than Allegheny Cemetery was becoming apparent.

Unlike Allegheny Cemetery, The Homewood Cemetery was, from the start, designed as a lawn park cemetery. Beginning in the 1850s, Prussian landscape architect Adolphe Strauch had conceived of a design that would replace ornate fencing and winding paths with open lots and structured roadways. Many of the varied plantings that had once dotted cemeteries were intentionally left out in order to open vistas and to encompass a clean view of the landscape. From its inception, The Homewood Cemetery embraced this concept—a simplified, streamlined, open design that allowed for a more strictly conceptualized layout for all to enjoy.

With this goal in mind, The Homewood Cemetery hired William Allen, who would become its superintendent from 1907 to 1935. Allen had firsthand experience with rural cemetery design, having worked at the celebrated Mount Auburn Cemetery in Cambridge, Massachusetts, which had been the first of its kind. While he remained focused on the natural layout of the cemetery, Allen was responsible for incorporating much of the landscape design in the trees throughout the grounds, although some original trees from the Wilkins estate remained when the grounds were initially cleared.

On September 19, 1878, Dr. John J. Marchand and his daughter Mardie became the first and second burials at The Homewood Cemetery, having been disinterred from their original burial plot at Allegheny Cemetery once space became available. Prior to the founding of The Homewood Cemetery, options for burials in the area were limited to several small cemeteries and very few large ones. Many families who had only recently moved to the East End chose to purchase large family plots at The Homewood Cemetery and soon coalesced family members from varying cemeteries into a single family estate. Judge William Wilkins was originally buried at Allegheny Cemetery, but his remains were returned to his original homestead in this manner to be buried in the newly constructed Wilkins family mausoleum (Section 4) in 1881.

From that day to this one, although much has changed in the communities surrounding The Homewood Cemetery, the grounds themselves remain much as they were when the cemetery was founded in 1878. A thick copse of trees still provides respite on hot summer days. Natural springs still feed the pond just inside where the gates now stand. An abundance of wildlife, such as red-tailed hawks, deer, groundhogs, and songbirds, still dot the grounds on crisp winter mornings when the snow falls silently among the tombstones.

In 2014, The Homewood Cemetery received the rare honor and recognition of becoming one of only 23 cemeteries (at the time) officially declared to be an arboretum. The designation came on behalf of the ArbNet Arboretum Accreditation Program and the Morton Arboretum. The honor was in specific recognition of over 40 species of trees within the grounds, including mature oak trees, flowering maples, and majestic horse chestnuts, among other notable specimens.

Over 78,000 souls lie at rest within these bucolic grounds. It is impossible to capture a fraction of even one of those lives within the confines of these pages. However, it is the hope of the author to bring to light the smallest part of these stories, which represent so many more that are untold. In reading these pages and remembering these names, we bring to life that which is gone, honor those who have served, and give voice to those who may have lacked it in their lifetimes.

Although this book cannot nearly encapsulate these legacies, you are most humbly invited to come and stroll the grounds alongside them, take in the rich sense of history, and walk amongst the many stories in the stones of The Homewood Cemetery.

One

A STROLL THROUGH THE STONES

Just beyond the hustle and bustle of the city of Pittsburgh lies the bucolic neighborhood of Point Breeze. The streets here teem with lives that have inherited a storied past. Steps away from the homes, businesses, and shops are the gates of The Homewood Cemetery. Prior to the cemetery's founding in 1878, these grounds served as the estate of William Wilkins and his family. Wilkins was well-known throughout the community for being a lawyer, civil servant, and prominent citizen. His family's estate, Homewood, was the namesake for the cemetery. When Wilkins died in 1865, he was buried at Allegheny Cemetery. Soon after his death, the land upon which his estate sat was sold for use as the primary resting space in Pittsburgh's East End. With this new burying ground available, Wilkins and other deceased members of his family were relocated from Allegheny Cemetery to his familial grounds. The family is now at rest in Section 4, near the main gates of The Homewood Cemetery. After the grounds were converted to a burial space, much was needed in terms of construction. Roadways were cleared, structures—such as the gatehouse and chapel—were built, and several public mausoleums were designed and constructed in order to respectfully accommodate the growing city's dead. The Homewood Cemetery is fortunate to have in its archives many images featuring that construction and progress phase. Amongst the images collected herein are those found on glass plate negatives that had been stored in the attic of the cemetery's administration building for decades. They were boxed and carefully protected but laid unnoticed until they were rediscovered by cemetery employees. Several of these images are being published for the first time. This chapter traverses the quiet paths, rolling hillsides, and serene natural springs that embody the history just inside the gates. Please join in this stroll through the stones.

HOMEWOOD. The grounds on which The Homewood Cemetery now stand once belonged to Judge William Wilkins of Pittsburgh. In the early 1830s, Judge Wilkins began construction on a homestead for his family that he would later name Homewood. This grand home sat among others of the era, including Henry Clay Frick's Clayton, George Westinghouse's Solitude, and H.J. Heinz's Greenlawn. The Homewood estate was ultimately demolished in 1924. (Courtesy of the Archives Service Center, University of Pittsburgh.)

REFLECTIONS IN TIME. Spanning both centuries and the vast expanse just inside the South Dallas Avenue gate, the natural spring pond shown here reflects the beauty and solitude of winter against the backdrop of the cemetery office. The cornerstone of the office building was laid by William H. Rea on July 9, 1886. This office was replaced when the new office was built in the 1920s. (Courtesy of The Homewood Cemetery.)

THE LAWN PARK CEMETERY DESIGN. This view from just inside the South Dallas Avenue gates shows the 1886 office integrated with natural ponds and gently sloping hillsides. Landscape architect Adolphe Strauch first designed the concept of a lawn park cemetery, focusing more on the nature of the grounds and less on the structures within them. Fences and decorative plantings were cleared to make way for a more uniform design. The lawn park layout was incorporated into The Homewood Cemetery from its beginning in 1878. (Courtesy of The Homewood Cemetery.)

SAMUEL YELLIN. Renowned metalworker Samuel Yellin began his training in Europe and later opened his own metalworking shop in Philadelphia. The Homewood Cemetery is fortunate to contain several examples of Yellin's work, including these fine iron gates that brace the South Dallas Avenue entrance. (Courtesy of The Homewood Cemetery.)

11

OFFICE BUILDING. Constructed in 1886, this served as an office building and the residence of the sexton from the late 19th century through the beginning of the 20th century. In the 1920s, it was moved across the street to make way for the current office building. This building remains standing but is now a private residence. (Courtesy of The Homewood Cemetery.)

FORBES ENTRANCE. This undated photograph from the cemetery's archives shows the view just outside of the Forbes Avenue entrance. These gates have welcomed visitors to the cemetery since the earliest days of the 20th century. (Courtesy of The Homewood Cemetery.)

STEWARDSHIP AND HONOR. Protecting the sanctity of the final resting place of so many, The Homewood Cemetery policeman John Swanson is pictured here in the early 1930s along with his police-issued 1932 Indian Chief motorcycle and sidecar. (Courtesy of The Homewood Cemetery.)

CHAPEL WINDOW. Dedicated in 1923, the chapel at The Homewood Cemetery features this stunning stained-glass window. The window was designed by George Green and crafted by Rudy Brothers of Pittsburgh. (Courtesy of The Homewood Cemetery.)

THE RUSSIAN COTTAGE. This 1854 painting by R. Cowan is believed to show the Russian cottage that once stood on the grounds and predated the Homewood mansion that belonged to Judge William Wilkins and for which The Homewood Cemetery was eventually named. (Courtesy of The Homewood Cemetery.)

FLORAL TRIBUTE. This image dating from the 1920s shows a floral tribute and cemetery superintendent William Allen. The image was discovered within a box of nearly century-old glass plate negatives that had been carefully stored in the rafters of the attic in the cemetery's administration building. (Courtesy of The Homewood Cemetery.)

A Chapel Funeral. The Homewood Cemetery features its own intimate chapel, located near the 1924 office complex. For almost 100 years, the chapel has hosted community events, weddings, memorial services, and funerals. The intricately carved dark wood is complemented by the abundance of light pouring through the central stained-glass window. This undated image is from The Homewood Cemetery archives. (Courtesy of The Homewood Cemetery.)

Barns (Erected 1909). Then as now, an essential function of cemetery maintenance is proper care for the grounds, flora, and fauna. This 1912 image shows one of the cemetery's maintenance barns, which still stands today. (Courtesy of The Homewood Cemetery.)

SECTION 20 POND. The Homewood Cemetery was initially designed as a lawn park cemetery by landscape architect Hamilton Shepherd. The artificial pond shown here was incorporated into the landscape of Section 20 to provide a peaceful place of respite for both the living and the dead. This pond no longer remains; however, it was located near where the newly created Posner Pond resides today. (Courtesy of The Homewood Cemetery.)

A BYGONE VIEW. This image shows another view of the pond in Section 20. As essential factors in lawn park cemetery design, ponds and lakes such as this were designed to enhance the deep vistas of the landscape. They placed the emphasis on the sky, light, and air and embraced the natural surroundings. This pond was filled in 1952, but the pond near the South Dallas Avenue entrance still remains and is fed by a natural spring on the cemetery grounds. (Courtesy of The Homewood Cemetery.)

THE STERRETT SCHOOL. Built in 1840 on the grounds of what is now The Homewood Cemetery, the Sterrett School has been a staple of the community for more than 175 years. In 1899, a second Sterrett School was built nearby, and it is shown in this photograph taken in the school's garden in 1917. (Courtesy of the Library of Congress.)

A LAWN PARK CEMETERY. The early 1800s saw the design of Romantic landscape-type cemeteries throughout the East Coast of the United States. When The Homewood Cemetery opened in 1878, it had a lawn park design, which eliminated the large structural encumbrances that made cemeteries difficult to maintain. Instead, the lawn park design focused on a strict layout while simultaneously integrating bucolic surroundings of hills, ravines, trees, and natural springs. Within this landscape, families could find peace and solace while the functional needs of the grounds remained incorporated. (Courtesy of the Library of Congress.)

1886 OFFICE BUILDING/1905 SEXTON'S RESIDENCE. Shown in a photograph from a 1905 cemetery publication, this building served as the first office of The Homewood Cemetery after it opened in 1878. It later served as the home of the cemetery's sexton—a role that now belongs to the cemetery's superintendent. (Courtesy of The Homewood Cemetery.)

FRICK FAMILY MONUMENT. In this image from a 1905 cemetery publication, the Frick family monument is pictured shortly after it was installed. In subsequent years, smaller family stones would adorn the plot to mark the passing of individual family members, such as Henry, Adelaide, and their children. The sweeping view shown here is now filled with mature trees that have grown around the family's plot over the 100-plus years since this marker was originally placed. (Courtesy of The Homewood Cemetery.)

COLUMBARIUM ENTRANCE, 1923.
This photograph from a glass
plate negative in the cemetery's
archives shows the columbarium
entrance flanked by a striking
glass window. This architecture
is representative of the gatehouse
complex that was built during the
early part of the 1920s. (Courtesy
of The Homewood Cemetery.)

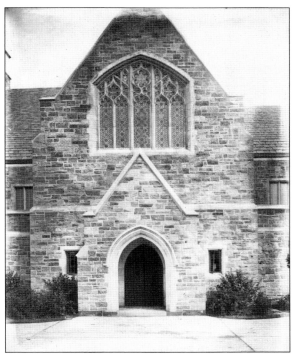

CEMETERY ROAD SECTION DEVELOPMENT. Although undated, this image is perhaps one of the
earliest from The Homewood Cemetery archives. The unidentified gentleman at left, in a top
hat and tie, provides a stark contrast to the workers behind him, who are shown clearing a road
with bare hands and wooden tools as a horse and cart remove the efforts of their labor. (Courtesy
of The Homewood Cemetery.)

BOARD OF MANAGERS, 1923. The 1923 board of managers for The Homewood Cemetery is pictured here nearly 50 years after the cemetery opened in 1878. Pictured are, from left to right: (first row) Charles Dickey Armstrong, James Ross Mellon, and George Davison; (second row) Howard Noble, W.W. Blackburn, William H. Rea, and Daniel Clemson. (Courtesy of The Homewood Cemetery.)

RECEIVING VAULTS AND COLUMBARIUM. The intricate stone archways and tranquil design of this columbarium are accented by ironwork gates designed by Samuel Yellin. Vaults like this one, which is within the administration building, offer an alternative to those who prefer above-ground burial. (Courtesy of The Homewood Cemetery.)

CHAPEL INTERIOR. This serene view from the interior of the cemetery's chapel looks much the same today as it did when the chapel was built in the 1920s. The space serves numerous purposes, including as a venue for services and community events. It remains a place of quiet reflection and reverence for all who seek solace within its doors. (Courtesy of The Homewood Cemetery.)

MAUSOLEUMS. Many prominent Pittsburgh families chose The Homewood Cemetery as their final resting place. Although many of these date to the early 20th century, the names—such as Barleigh, Bigelow, Pitcairn, and Jennings (the mausoleums shown here)—are still recognized today in neighborhoods and along transportation routes throughout the city. (Courtesy of The Homewood Cemetery.)

EAST UNIT MAUSOLEUM. This peaceful vista and eternal flame grace the entrance of the East Unit Mausoleum, which serves as a prime example of the seamless integration of the cemetery's structures within its surrounding nature. Both are embraced in order to provide a sense of welcoming and comfort to visiting families. (Courtesy of The Homewood Cemetery.)

CEMETERY GROUNDS, 1920s. Prior to the advent of more technically advanced alternatives, much of the maintenance of cemetery grounds utilized manual labor provided by cemetery employees and teams of horses and carts dedicated to tasks such as clearing roads, forging new paths, and the general upkeep of the grounds. (Courtesy of The Homewood Cemetery.)

GATEHOUSE EXTERIOR. This image shows just how little the facade of The Homewood Cemetery has changed over the last century. Although this dates from the 1920s, one would find the same view standing before these gates today. While the city of Pittsburgh has developed and changed around it, the grounds of The Homewood Cemetery remain a respite from an ever-changing world. (Courtesy of The Homewood Cemetery.)

IVY FRAMES AND GREENHOUSES. Six greenhouses, a palm house, and the ivy frames pictured here once graced the grounds of The Homewood Cemetery. None remain today. When the last of the six greenhouses was dismantled in the 1990s, Pittsburgh's Phipps Conservatory acquired several pieces of the hardware and framework, as both the last remaining greenhouse at The Homewood Cemetery and the Phipps Conservatory Greenhouse dated to the same period of initial construction. (Courtesy of The Homewood Cemetery.)

MALCOLM HAY MONUMENT. This stunning and intricately carved Celtic cross commemorates Malcolm Hay (1842–1885) and his wife, Virginia Eleanor Hay (1845–1913). Born in Philadelphia and New York, respectively, both died in Pittsburgh, as noted on the monument. The detailing concludes with a quote conveying finality: "God shall wipe away all the tears from their eyes. The righteous shall be had in everlasting remembrance." (Courtesy of The Homewood Cemetery.)

ON THE MOVE. When the cemetery's new office complex was built in the early 1920s, the original office (pictured) was moved across the street, where it remains as a residence. Note the female crane operator—a rarity. She is Jane Shilladay, stepdaughter of John Eichleay Jr., the man who owned the construction company responsible for moving the original office to its new location. (Courtesy of The Homewood Cemetery.)

RECEIVING VAULT. Receiving vaults, such as this one at The Homewood Cemetery pictured in a 1905 cemetery publication, were used for a number of different purposes. When the grounds were too frozen for burials, the receiving vault would serve as a temporary crypt. During times of epidemics or disasters, it could be used to accommodate a large number of remains until families could arrange for burials. (Courtesy of The Homewood Cemetery.)

THE CHINESE CEMETERY. In 1901, the Chinese Cemetery Association founded the Chinese Cemetery within The Homewood Cemetery. The association procured additional sections in 1903, 1918, and 1929 and likely hosted Chinese funerals such as this one. In 2018, a generous grant from the Hillman Foundation provided for the restoration of these monuments. Today, it is one of the oldest Chinese cemeteries on the East Coast. (Courtesy of the Library of Congress.)

BIGELOW FAMILY MAUSOLEUM, SECTION 14. The Bigelow family left an indelible mark on the city of Pittsburgh. Edward Manning Bigelow (1850–1916) was a city planner whose legacy is best encapsulated by his efforts to secure Schenley and Highland Parks. Both parks remain integral parts of Pittsburgh to this day. The Bigelow mausoleum is shown here in an image from a 1912 cemetery publication. (Courtesy of The Homewood Cemetery.)

WEST UNIT MAUSOLEUM CONSTRUCTION, SEPTEMBER 1940. During the first half of the 20th century, construction efforts began to ensure an adequate and respectful place for future needs. This image shows the construction of the East Wing of the West Unit Mausoleum, which still stands today. The doorway at far left remains the main entrance, while the three windows around the corner from the doorway are now an additional entryway. (Courtesy of The Homewood Cemetery.)

FIXED IN CONCRETE, 1950s. Construction has been ongoing throughout the 140-plus years of The Homewood Cemetery's existence. Here, cemetery employees Jim Haith (left) and Joe Swift prepare to mix a batch of cement to assist with one of the many projects of the time. (Courtesy of The Homewood Cemetery.)

THE HOMEWOOD CEMETERY'S FIRST BACKHOE, 1952. Routine cemetery maintenance changed in the years following World War II. What was once done by hand could now be done with the help of the cemetery's first backhoe. Cemetery foreman Jack Mullen (right) and Juan Bogovich are shown braving a snowy landscape against the backdrop of local communities. (Courtesy of The Homewood Cemetery.)

EAST UNIT MAUSOLEUM CONSTRUCTION (EXTERIOR). Before the interior construction could take place, the exterior of the East Unit Mausoleum had to be completed. Despite the foreboding winter climate, these exterior walls and framing began to take shape in the winter of 1946. (Courtesy of The Homewood Cemetery.)

EAST UNIT MAUSOLEUM CONSTRUCTION (INTERIOR). The beginning of 1949 brought many changes to The Homewood Cemetery. Specifically, construction was underway on the East Unit Mausoleum. The units at right are now used as double-depth crypts. Note the size of the jacket and hat at right and the man to the left of the scaffolding that indicate the scale of the construction project. (Courtesy of The Homewood Cemetery.)

CREMATORY CONSTRUCTION.
Construction of the cemetery's crematory took place in the mid-20th century. The process involved great coordination in terms of both labor and equipment. This tubular tower shovel was used for pouring the concrete that would eventually compose the second floor of the building. (Courtesy of The Homewood Cemetery.)

CONSTRUCTION PROGRESSES. Workmen are shown during the construction of the cemetery's crematory. As more families requested cremation, the crematory allowed for the cemetery to accommodate those requests with the utmost dignity for families. (Courtesy of The Homewood Cemetery.)

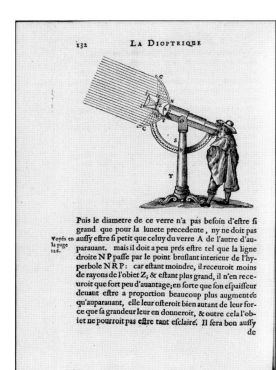

132　　　LA DIOPTRIQUE

Puis le diametre de ce verre n'a pas befoin d'eftre fi grand que pour la lunete precedente , ny ne doit pas Voyés en auffy eftre fi petit que celuy du verre A de l'autre d'au-la page parauant. mais il doit a peu prés eftre tel que la ligne 126. droite N P paffe par le point bruflant interieur de l'hy-perbole N R P : car eftant moindre, il receuroit moins de rayons de l'obiet Z; & eftant plus grand, il n'en rece-uroit que fort peu d'auantage; en forte que fon efpaiffeur deuant eftre a proportion beaucoup plus augmentée qu'auparauant, elle leur ofteroit bien autant de leur for-ce que fa grandeur leur en donneroit, & outre cela l'ob-iet ne pourroit pas eftre tant efclairé. Il fera bon auffy de

OUT OF THIS WORLD. An unexpected visitor arrived near the gates of The Homewood Cemetery in August 1904. The *Pittsburgh Gazette* described "a burst of light more intense than the skill of man has yet devised." A four-foot-square meteor rushed toward the gates with its tail visible over the cemetery. Passersby heard the sound of a loud explosion as the mass neared the ground and fragmented into dust before their eyes. (Courtesy of the Library of Congress.)

LIGHTNING CRASHES, 1940. The July 9, 1940, *Pittsburgh Post-Gazette* noted a "special report from the United States Weather Bureau" calling for "mostly cloudy and probably thunderstorms today." On that day, an explosive force, later revealed to be lightning, struck the cemetery's chimney, scattering stones across the rooftop below it. The damage was repaired, but fortunately, this image documenting the event remains. (Courtesy of The Homewood Cemetery.)

Two

TITANS OF THEIR TIME

The giants of industry, civil service, and Pittsburgh politics have names that are instantly recognizable. To this day, they are written on the city's infrastructure in schools, parks, charities, and streets. One may recall names such as Dilworth, Herron, Pitcairn, Bigelow, Flinn, Wilkins, Mellon, Frick, Hillman, Benedum, and Heinz. Many of these names are associated with the rising industrialism of Pittsburgh at the end of the 19th century. As the city grew, so did its foundations. Civic planning led to the establishment of main thoroughfares that traverse the city. Parks and green spaces were preserved and designed well ahead of their time. Several Pittsburgh corporations were developed in their earliest iterations, and legacies began that would last many lifetimes. In terms of corporate development, the city was on the forefront of manufacturing and production. This resulted in the growth of banks and financial institutions throughout the city. Tied in with the burgeoning financial sector were many prominent attorneys, politicians, and civil servants. Each of the great industries of this city seemed tied to the rise of another, and as they grew, so did the fortunes of individuals and the city as a whole. By the turn of the 20th century, several of the individuals who had first gained prominence locally were becoming known nationwide—even worldwide. Their significant contributions have rippled through the decades and centuries, and many of them are still notable to this day. Some started small, others loomed large, but all are associated with the fabric that is woven into the history of Pittsburgh. Many of those who created these legacies are now at rest within The Homewood Cemetery and remembered as titans of their time.

HENRY CLAY FRICK (DIED 1919; SECTION 14). Henry Clay Frick is one of the people who built Pittsburgh. He served in numerous capacities throughout his lifetime, including as head of H.C. Frick & Company (a coke manufacturer), chairman of Carnegie Steel Company, heir to the Overholt whiskey corporation, and renowned art collector. He was also one of the founding members of the South Fork Fishing and Hunting Club. In 1881, he married Adelaide Howard Childs, and they had four children. In 1892, Frick survived an assassination attempt in his private office. In 1912, Henry and Adelaide purchased tickets to return to the United States aboard the *Titanic* after a visit to Italy—a trip they missed only because Adelaide sprained her ankle, saving both of them from an unknown fate. (Courtesy of the Library of Congress.)

CHILDS FRICK (DIED 1965; SECTION 14). The first of the Frick children, Childs spent his early years on the grounds of the family home, Clayton, just outside Pittsburgh. Those days were formative, and his love of the nature surrounding the home eventually led to a career as a paleontologist and trustee for the American Museum of Natural History. He procured hundreds of thousands of specimens, which he then donated to the museum's collection. He and his wife, Frances Shoemaker Dixon, had four children. (Courtesy of the Frick Collection/Frick Art Reference Library Archives.)

DAVID LYTLE CLARK (DIED 1939; SECTION 25). Born in Ireland in 1864, David L. Clark became an entrepreneur and confectioner. The D.L. Clark Company was best known for its signature products, the Clark Bar and the Zagnut Bar. (Courtesy of The Homewood Cemetery.)

GEORGE WASHINGTON DILWORTH (DIED 1900; SECTION 4). Along with his brother Joseph, George W. Dilworth was one of the founding members of the Dilworth Brothers dry goods operation, one of the premier wholesalers not only in Pittsburgh but on the entire East Coast of the United States. At the time of his death, George was one of the oldest members of the Duquesne Club and also its president. He was survived by his wife, Mary, and their three children. (Courtesy of Jamie Edwards.)

ABRAHAM LINCOLN once said:

"YOU MAY FOOL ALL THE PEOPLE SOME OF THE TIME, AND SOME OF THE PEOPLE ALL THE TIME, BUT YOU CAN-NOT FOOL ALL THE PEOPLE ALL THE TIME."

DON'T BE FOOLED ALL THE TIME by alleged mixtures of expensive coffees which are offered at same prices as our brand. There is not enough Java and Mocha brought to this country to furnish one-fourth the roasted coffee so branded. Don't encourage fraudulent branding or advertising.

DON'T BE FOOLED ALL THE TIME with inferior coffee promoted by prize or lottery schemes. The consumer always pays for such in-ducements. It cannot be otherwise.

Don't use an old coffee-pot which has lost its inside coating of tin. Good coffee is utterly ruined by brewing it in such a vessel.

DILWORTH BROTHERS,
PITTSBURGH.

If you want a handsome Iron Chest to protect household goods, grain, seeds, etc., from rats and mice, ask your grocer for one of

DILWORTH'S SAFE STORAGE CHESTS,
PRICE, $1.50.

DILWORTH BROTHERS. Known under several different names, Dilworth Brothers became a well-known distributor of dry goods in Pittsburgh's Strip District neighborhood. George W. Dilworth was a founding member of the company in 1871 along with his brother Joseph. The company sold numerous products, including coffee, storage chests, and other wholesale goods. (Courtesy of The Homewood Cemetery.)

JOHN EATON (DIED 1912; SECTION 14). Capitalist John Eaton was a titan of Pittsburgh manufacturing circles in the early part of the 20th century. He served in several capacities, including as president of the Pittsburgh Chamber of Commerce, president of the Oil Well Supply Company, and director of the Kingsley House Association. (Courtesy of The Homewood Cemetery.)

ADAM BROWN (DIED 1901; SECTION 15). Anchor Savings Bank was one of the best-known banks in Pittsburgh during the latter part of the 19th century. It was a time of prosperity in the city, and banking was every bit the successful industry that manufacturing had become. Brown served as president of Anchor Savings Bank and was successful in both business and politics. He was a leading member of the bar association and had the distinguished honor of being the first recorder for the City of Pittsburgh. (Courtesy of The Homewood Cemetery.)

JAMES BENIJAH COREY (DIED 1921; SECTION 10). As Pittsburgh's manufacturing needs boomed, so did the city's need for fuel sources such as oil and gas. James Benijah Corey, a captain of industry, founded J.B. Corey & Company, working with several partners to transport coal along the rivers. He later served as the director of the Braddock National Bank. (Courtesy of The Homewood Cemetery.)

WILLIAM H. SCHOEN (DIED 1923; SECTION 4). William Schoen was a representative of several Pittsburgh iron and steel manufacturers. When he arrived in Pittsburgh in 1890, he established the Schoen Pressed Steel Company with an uncle. He remained an astute businessman, and at the time of his death, he was president and director of numerous Pittsburgh manufacturing companies. (Courtesy of The Homewood Cemetery.)

HENRY GOURLEY (DIED 1899; SECTION 6). The son of a poor peasant family from Juniata County, Pennsylvania, Henry Gourley was raised on a farm in Pine Township just outside of Pittsburgh. Gourley spent a portion of his life working as a schoolteacher. He subsequently entered civil service when he was elected to Pittsburgh's city council in 1876. Well respected and highly reputable, Gourley was selected as the 35th mayor of Pittsburgh in 1890. He held that role for three years and was serving as the city controller at the time of his death in 1899. (Courtesy of The Homewood Cemetery.)

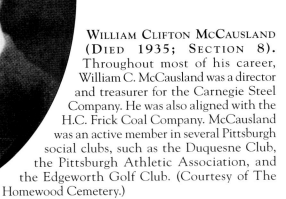

WILLIAM CLIFTON McCAUSLAND (DIED 1935; SECTION 8). Throughout most of his career, William C. McCausland was a director and treasurer for the Carnegie Steel Company. He was also aligned with the H.C. Frick Coal Company. McCausland was an active member in several Pittsburgh social clubs, such as the Duquesne Club, the Pittsburgh Athletic Association, and the Edgeworth Golf Club. (Courtesy of The Homewood Cemetery.)

SEN. WILLIAM FLINN (DIED 1924; SECTION 14). The son of English and Irish immigrants, William Flinn (at left, wearing a hat and glasses) raised himself up from only a secondary education to eventually become a titan of the business world. Beginning in 1876, he found work as a general contractor. This led to the founding of the Booth & Flinn Construction Company just a few years later. The company built such notable projects as the Holland Tunnel in New York and the Liberty, Wabash, and Armstrong Tunnels in Pittsburgh. Senator Flinn married Nancy Galbraith in 1874, and the couple had seven children. He quietly contributed to philanthropic causes throughout his life, including the Magee and West Penn Hospitals. Flinn also maintained a close personal friendship with Teddy Roosevelt, with whom he is pictured at an event in 1917. (Courtesy of Hartwood Mansion.)

THE BONDS OF BROTHERHOOD. With World War I raging throughout Europe, three Flinn brothers—the sons of Sen. William Flinn—answered the call to defend their country. William Arthur (left), Ralph Emerson (center), and A. Rex Flinn fought to preserve the rights and welfare of those affected by the horrors of the war. William Arthur Flinn was called into service as a first lieutenant in an Aero Squadron and the American Expeditionary Forces and lived in Greenwich, Connecticut, after returning to civilian life. Ralph Emerson Flinn served in the US Army during World War I and World War II. A World War I US Army Transport Service passenger list indicates that Capt. A. Rex Flinn returned home to his wife, Eleanor, in March 1919 after serving in the 2nd Battalion, 106th Field Artillery, 27th Division. The three brothers posed for this photograph before joining the war, and each survived to tell his stories after it was over. (Courtesy of Hartwood Mansion.)

GEORGE MESTA (DIED 1925; SECTION 21). George Mesta founded Mesta Machinery in 1898. The company focused on steel manufacturing and had factories across the world. During wartime, the company's factories produced guns, cannons, ship machinery, and mortar shells. Mesta died in 1925, but the company persisted until its last assets were sold in 1988. (Courtesy of the Library of Congress.)

AUGUST E. SUCCOP (DIED 1931; SECTION 16). Described in the 1913 *Book of Prominent Pennsylvanians* as "importantly connected," A.E. Succop was primarily a banker who held positions with the Germania Savings Bank, German Fire Insurance Company, Columbia National Bank, Colonial Trust Company, Freehold Bank, Parkersburg Iron and Steel Company, and Manufacturers Light and Heat Company. He was also a member of several notable social clubs, including the Duquesne Club, the Pittsburgh Country Club, and the German Club. (Courtesy of The Homewood Cemetery.)

WALLACE H. ROWE (DIED 1919; SECTION 14). Best known for his work in Pittsburgh's steel industry, Wallace Rowe was involved with several notable businesses throughout his lifetime. He initially worked in the banking industry alongside his father. In 1886, he moved to Pittsburgh and accepted a position as the treasurer and general manager of the Braddock Wire Company, which was absorbed into the US Steel Company in 1901. Rowe's obituary also notes his dedicated involvement with Pittsburgh's Children's Hospital and the Western Pennsylvania Institution for the Blind. (Courtesy of The Homewood Cemetery.)

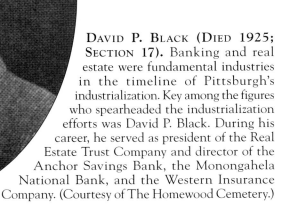

DAVID P. BLACK (DIED 1925; SECTION 17). Banking and real estate were fundamental industries in the timeline of Pittsburgh's industrialization. Key among the figures who spearheaded the industrialization efforts was David P. Black. During his career, he served as president of the Real Estate Trust Company and director of the Anchor Savings Bank, the Monongahela National Bank, and the Western Insurance Company. (Courtesy of The Homewood Cemetery.)

41

HENRY CLAY BAIR (DIED 1922; SECTION 8). Henry Clay Bair was a Civil War veteran who served with Company D, 122nd Pennsylvania Infantry. After his military service, he became a founding member and president of the Bair and Gazzam Manufacturing Company. Additionally, he was a director of the Fort Pitt and Commercial National Banks and the Commonwealth Trust Company. (Courtesy of The Homewood Cemetery.)

THOMAS MORRISON (DIED 1946; SECTION 14). Along with many other giants of the time, Thomas Morrison was a captain of Pittsburgh's industry as it boomed at the beginning of the 20th century. First serving as general superintendent of the Duquesne Works, Morrison later held the position of general superintendent of the Edgar Thompson Works. His prestigious home, Rhu-Na-Craig, sat along North Highland Avenue in Pittsburgh's Highland Park neighborhood. (Courtesy of The Homewood Cemetery.)

ROBERT L. VANN (DIED 1941; SECTION 21). In 1910, Robert Vann was one of only five African American attorneys in the city of Pittsburgh. This notable achievement would not be his best-known legacy. That same year, Vann incorporated the *Pittsburgh Courier*, a weekly African American–focused newspaper that often covered hardships and adversity faced by minorities. It was in circulation until the mid-1960s throughout the United States as well as internationally. (Courtesy of the Library of Congress.)

WILLIAM LARIMER MELLON (DIED 1949; SECTION 14). The son of James Ross Mellon and Rachel Larimer Mellon, William Larimer Mellon had an interest in the oil industry from a young age. He established his own company, which was subsequently acquired by Rockefeller's Standard Oil in 1895. He later founded Gulf Oil along with his uncle Andrew Mellon. Additionally, Mellon served as the chairman for the Pennsylvania Republican Party during the late 1920s. (Courtesy of The Homewood Cemetery.)

HENRY JOHN HEINZ (DIED 1919; SECTION 14). In 1869, Henry Heinz founded what would become a world-famous food company known for its "57 Varieties." Recognized for both the quality of its products and its numerous successful marketing techniques (such as the Heinz Pickle Pin), the company grew well beyond the 57 varieties and was one of the few food manufacturers that supported the 1906 Pure Food and Drug Act. Heinz factories were open to tour and exemplified cleanliness and ingenuity rarely seen in that era. In 1869, he married Sarah (pictured here with Henry on their wedding trip). The couple had five children prior to Sarah's death in 1894. (Courtesy of the Library of Congress.)

JOHN HEINZ III (DIED 1991; SECTION 14). Businessman John Heinz III, great-grandson of Henry John Heinz, had success in his blood. He was well-known as a scion of the Heinz family. After graduating from Yale and Harvard, he spent time with the US Air Force Reserve. For a short time, Heinz took on a role in the family business, and he later became a professor at Carnegie Mellon University. In 1971, Heinz entered the political arena when he ran for an empty seat in Pennsylvania's 18th Congressional District. He won and was subsequently re-elected twice. In 1976, he won a seat in the US Senate. Sadly, in 1991, Heinz was killed as the result of a tragic air accident, and he now rests in the Heinz family mausoleum at The Homewood Cemetery. The family mausoleum was designed by Vrydaugh & Wolfe, the same architects who designed the H.J. Heinz family estate, Greenlawn. (Courtesy of Becca Taylor.)

HENRY HILLMAN (DIED 2017; SECTION 25). Success can be defined by professional and personal accomplishments. Henry Hillman had an abundance of both. A driving force in Pittsburgh's industrial renaissance of the 1940s, Hillman served with Pittsburgh Coke, Pittsburgh National Bank/PNC, and many other companies throughout the region. He utilized that professional success to better the community around him. His philanthropic efforts benefited organizations such as Pittsburgh's Children's Hospital, the Carnegie Hero Fund, the Carnegie Museum, and the Hillman Cancer Center, among others, and led to Hillman receiving numerous honors and awards. (Courtesy of the Hillman Foundation.)

WILLIAM HARRY BROWN AND FAMILY (DIED 1921; SECTION 14). One of the most recognizable monuments in The Homewood Cemetery is the pyramid memorializing William H. Brown and his family. The Browns operated one of the largest coal-shipping businesses of the time on the Ohio and Mississippi Rivers. They were well traveled and enjoyed exotic trips, like this visit to the Sphinx and the Egyptian pyramids around the end of the 19th century. The influence of that trip on the family was so great that they were eventually buried in this pyramid replica designed by the well-known architecture firm Alden & Harlow. (Both, courtesy of The Homewood Cemetery.)

WILLIAM A. HERRON (DIED 1889; SECTION 3). The Herron name is noted throughout the streets of Pittsburgh. William Herron is the main reason for that. He subdivided what was then known as Herron Hill, which was once home to three family farms dating to the 1700s, into areas such as Springfield Farms and the Hill District. He was also responsible for subdividing much of what are now the Schenley Farms, Shadyside, and Oakland neighborhoods of Pittsburgh. His civil service later expanded, and Herron became a founder of Commonwealth Bank. The only known color image of him—a painting done during his lifetime—is now on display at the Detre Library & Archives at the Heinz History Center. (Courtesy of Becca Taylor.)

HOWARD HALE MCCLINTIC (DIED 1938; SECTION 14). The accomplishments of Howard McClintic, cofounder of the McClintic-Marshall Construction Company in 1900, were known worldwide. The company produced structural steel that was used to build the Empire State Building, Panama Canal, and the Golden Gate Bridge. In 1931, industry giant Bethlehem Steel acquired the company for $32 million. Aside from these notable achievements, McClintic served as a member of the Carnegie Hero Fund Commission from 1912 until his death, after which he was succeeded by his son, Stewart McClintic. (Courtesy of the Library of Congress.)

SARAH, CLAUDE, AND MICHAEL BENEDUM (PRIVATE MAUSOLEUM; SECTION 14). Michael Late Benedum was one of the best-known oilmen in the Pittsburgh area. As half-owner of the Benedum Trees Company, he saw many successes throughout his lifetime. He and his wife, Sarah, started a family, and their son Claude was born in 1898. Just twenty years later, their son (by then a lieutenant in the military) was lost to the influenza pandemic that swept the world in 1918. When the Benedums passed in the 1950s, they left behind a foundation in their son's name that continues to flourish and enriches the city of Pittsburgh. (Courtesy of the Benedum Foundation.)

50

THOMAS M. ARMSTRONG (DIED 1908; SECTION 6). Thomas Armstrong's business started with only one partner (John Glass) in a small, one-room operation making cork bottle stoppers by hand. They had the foresight to brand the stoppers, making their business, Armstrong Cork Company, well-known. Within a few decades, that one-room endeavor was recognized worldwide, and the business branched out to manufacture building materials such as brick, linoleum, fiberboard, ceiling boards, vinyl tile, ceramic tile, and carpeting. Although the company has undergone several ownership changes, it is still in existence today, over a century and a half after it was founded. (Courtesy of The Homewood Cemetery.)

DAVID HERBERT HOSTETTER (DIED 1924; SECTION 14). David Herbert Hostetter was born in Allegheny in 1859. A legacy of prosperity was passed through three generations and eventually fell on his shoulders. His physician grandfather Jacob Hostetter and father, David Hostetter Sr., developed and distributed the recipe for a famous Civil War–era cure-all called Hostetter's Stomach Bitters. It was well-received and brought the family much fame and fortune. Upon the death of David Hostetter Sr., interests in the company transferred to his son David. Although the family conducted business in several prominent fields in Pittsburgh, such as oil, natural gas, banking, and the railroads, their largest success had been with Hostetter's Stomach Bitters. The popularity of the product made the Hostetter name known not only in the Pittsburgh area, where they resided, but throughout the country. (Courtesy of the Library of Congress.)

MME. CURIE

HENRY TITUS KOENIG (DIED 1934; SECTION 9). Known worldwide for his work with famed radium researcher Marie Curie (pictured), Henry Titus Koenig devoted his life to protecting the public from the negative fallout of this radioactive element. Along with a group of approximately 20 other scientists, Koenig utilized his expertise to investigate what had once been a cure-all but was quickly becoming a death sentence. He and the other scientists developed radium poisoning during the course of their work. He was the last of them to die, with Curie herself dying just two months later. Because of their diligent efforts, however, the world gained a greater understanding of the dangers of radium, and humanity was safer thanks to their contributions and sacrifices. (Courtesy of the Library of Congress.)

JAMES ROSS MELLON (DIED 1934; SECTION 14). Born a scion of the famous Mellon banking family, James Ross Mellon attended Jefferson College in Pennsylvania. He took a job in Milwaukee as a clerk and later returned to Pittsburgh by way of Leavenworth, Kansas, where he stopped on family business. There, he met Rachel Larimer, the woman he would marry in 1867. Upon his return to Pittsburgh, Mellon worked in the coal and lumber industries before founding City Deposit Bank & Trust Company with his brother Thomas in 1873. James remained there as bank president for the rest of his life. In addition, he worked with a number of other organizations, including the Western Pennsylvania Hospital, the East Liberty Presbyterian Church, and the Allegheny County Juvenile Court Farm. (Courtesy of The Homewood Cemetery.)

HILL BURGWIN (DIED 1898; SECTION 10). Hill Burgwin moved from North Carolina to Pennsylvania, establishing the first of many generations in the state. For more than 50 years, he served as a lawyer and prominent figure in the Allegheny County Bar. He was also an esteemed chancellor in the Episcopal Church and helped build the Church of the Good Shepherd in Hazelwood, Pennsylvania, which remains today. (Courtesy of Elizabeth Burgwin.)

AUGUSTUS PHILLIPS BURGWIN (DIED 1932; SECTION 10). The youngest son of Hill and Mary Burgwin, Augustus followed in his father's footsteps and pursued a legal career. He served as a major in the Judge Advocate General's Corps and was subsequently appointed special assistant US attorney. Augustus married Mildred Carlisle in 1893, and both are now at rest in The Homewood Cemetery. (Courtesy of Elizabeth Burgwin.)

WILLIAM WILKINS (DIED 1865; SECTION 4). The ground on which The Homewood Cemetery now stands was once the homestead of Judge William Wilkins. Throughout his lifetime, he served in many capacities, including judge, US senator, and, ultimately, secretary of war under President Tyler. Wilkins was married to Matilda Dallas, the namesake for South Dallas Avenue, where the cemetery is located. The family's mausoleum, located in Section 4 and designed as an homage to the tomb of King Mausolus, is the cemetery's oldest. (Courtesy of The Homewood Cemetery.)

EDWARD MANNING BIGELOW (DIED 1916; SECTION 14). Appointed city engineer in 1880, Edward Manning Bigelow oversaw much of the city's civic design during the peak of Pittsburgh's rise in industry. As factories choked the city, Bigelow recognized the need for public park spaces and worked diligently to secure them for the city. The land for Schenley Park and Highland Park was designated through his efforts. As a city planner, he also helped to design many of the main routes and thoroughfares that still cross the city. (Courtesy of The Homewood Cemetery.)

Ogden Methias Edwards (Died 1920; Section 14). A scion of one of Pittsburgh's oldest families, Ogden Edwards served in numerous directorial capacities throughout his lifetime. He was the founder of Edwards & Kenney, a leading insurance house in Pittsburgh during the mid-19th century. He also served as a director for the Western Pennsylvania Hospital and the Dixmont Hospital for the Insane in addition to being on the board of directors for the Western Pennsylvania Institution for the Blind (shown here). For 30 years, he was a member of the board of trustees for the Shadyside Presbyterian Church and served as a director of the Commonwealth Trust Company of Pittsburgh. He was survived by his widow, Sarah Herron Edwards, and three children. (Courtesy of the Library of Congress.)

ROBERT PITCAIRN (DIED 1909; SECTION 14). Just after noon on May 31, 1889, Robert Pitcairn received a telegram—"South Fork Dam liable to break." Within the hour, he rushed aboard his private train car, passing town after town in an attempt to get to the dam as soon as possible. He was too late. When he arrived, the dam had broken, and the devastation of the Johnstown Flood was beginning to unfold. Along with others, he jumped into the floodwaters to rescue victims but was powerless against the rapids. As a representative of the Pittsburgh Division of the Pennsylvania Railroad, Pitcairn had access to rail cars, which gave him a means to help evacuate the victims of the disaster. He instead turned to loading his train car with passengers, trying to take them from the chaotic melee to safety. He later spoke with firsthand knowledge of the disaster and made a concentrated effort to secure relief funding for the many who had suffered great losses. (Both, courtesy of The Homewood Cemetery.)

THE POSNER FAMILY. Henry Posner Jr. was a chemist and a businessman but perhaps will be best remembered for being a generous philanthropist alongside his wife, Helen. Posner's work as a research scientist led him to a position with the Manhattan Project, which helped develop the atomic bomb during World War II. After the war, he became head of Pittsburgh Outdoor Advertising Company, which had been his father's company; it was one of many he would lead throughout his lifetime. Henry and Helen donated millions to organizations that benefited Jewish communities worldwide, including those in the former Soviet Union. The Posners also contributed to several political campaigns, such as those of Pittsburgh mayor Tom Murphy and Allegheny County chief executive Jim Roddey, with whom he developed a close personal friendship. Preceded in death by one son, Henry Posner Jr. was survived by his wife, Helen; several sons; and many grandchildren. (Courtesy of Becca Taylor.)

WILLIAM H. MOORE

November 1, 1925 – August 6, 2007

Bill was the name his parents gave him,
Muggsy was the name he was often called by friends,
"Chief" was the name used by his staff and colleagues,
But Dad and Granddad were the names he treasured the most.

WILLIAM "MUGGSY" MOORE (DIED 2007; SECTION 33). As Pittsburgh's first African American police chief, Muggsy Moore knew struggle. He knew what it meant to strive for success in the face of the oppression that sought to hold him back. He overcame adversity and, in 1986, was appointed chief of police for the city of Pittsburgh by Mayor Richard Caliguiri. Understanding sociopolitical difficulties, Moore advocated for women and minorities on the police force, promoting individuals such as Pittsburgh's legendary Therese Rocco to the role of commander, making her the first woman to hold the position. As a police officer, Moore was known for being gritty, tough, resilient, and thorough. His personality served to solidify connections with people who ranged from hard-core individuals on the street to those in the corridors of city hall. Throughout his career that lasted for more than 35 years, Moore not only advocated for the rights of local minorities but for all minorities as a dedicated representative of the NAACP. He continued his police work throughout his life, also serving as the police chief for the Pittsburgh suburb of Braddock from 1991 to 1998. (Courtesy of Becca Taylor.)

DR. JAKE MILLIONES (DIED 1993; SECTION 33). "The Brother Was Deep"—this is the inscription that graces the eternal resting place of Dr. Jake Milliones. It doesn't even begin to cover the legacy he left behind. When Jake's wife, Margaret, a Pittsburgh Board of Public Education member, suddenly passed away, he stepped up to fill her shoes on the school board. As a grieving widower with four young children, he sought to better the education and community of Pittsburgh's children. He continued this work through his efforts with the Pittsburgh Peace Institute. When he was elected to Pittsburgh's city council, he tirelessly fought for the rights of local African American communities such as those in the Hill District and Northside. He pursued all of these efforts with a courageous heart and improved countless lives as a result of his tenacity and constant resolve. (Courtesy of Becca Taylor.)

NATE SMITH (DIED 2011; SECTION 29). As a strong and powerful voice for change in Pittsburgh's trade labor unions, Nate Smith put a lot on the line to demand progress. Perhaps he best demonstrated this by lying down in front of a bulldozer in 1969 during the construction of Three Rivers Stadium in an effort to bring focus to the lack of African American and female union workers on the project. In addition to undertaking such visceral protests, he worked with union leadership and Pittsburgh mayor Joseph Barr to bring focus to civil and political issues and effect the change that was so desperately needed. His tireless work and dedication earned him national acclaim, and he was honored by greats such as Rev. Jesse Jackson, Jimmy Carter, Gerald Ford, and George H.W. Bush, among countless others, for the social changes he fought to realize. (Courtesy of the Archives Service Center, University of Pittsburgh.)

Three

SERVICE AND SACRIFICE

Heroes are forged in the face of unthinkable chaos. They are the people who run in when anyone else would run out. Some live ordinary lives until they are called upon to serve. Others have service in their blood and are destined to safeguard the well-being of others. Mere words cannot justify the debt of gratitude owed to them. Within these pages lie stories from many conflicts spanning continents and decades. A single thread ties them all together: courage. Not all of these battles were fought on the front lines. Some of these heroes fought through endless hours of research to protect those who serve. Some fought through the heartbreaking and overwhelming loss of a child. Others fought for their country. Some trudged through hellish battles in the trenches of World War I, while others took to the skies to defend those who could not defend themselves. These are brothers, mothers, poet-warriors, and those who would never come home. As is easy to do amidst the immense loss of life that accompanies most wars, many of their names have been lost in the pages of history. Here, in this moment and in this time, pause to reflect on, honor, and remember just a few of the tales that remain to be told. These stories are presented in order to—in some small respect—thank these heroes for their service and sacrifice.

WENDELL FREELAND (DIED 2017; SECTION 12). There is no notation of Wendell Freeland's extraordinary military service on his headstone, only a small image of an airplane alongside his name. Freeland served as a member of the now famous and honored Tuskegee Airmen during World War II and took part in the Freeman Field Mutiny in 1945. This event, along with many others throughout his lifetime, exemplified his commitment to the civil rights movement. He focused his efforts on both current issues and historical ones, noting as one of his greatest achievements his campaign to have 19th-century lawyer George Vashon admitted to the bar. Freeland graduated from Howard University and the University of Maryland School of Law. As an attorney, he frequently worked with notable Pittsburgh icon Elsie Hillman and also handled many cases for underprivileged minorities, often pro bono. (Courtesy of Becca Taylor.)

WILLIAM FLINN II (DIED 1944). Pictured here with his crew, 1st Lt. William Flinn II (first row, center) served with the US Army Air Forces' 386th Bomb Group, 555th Bomb Squadron, in World War II. On October 5, 1944, Flinn piloted a B-26 called the "Yankee Guerrilla" on a covert mission to attack a German military location. On the return trip, the plane suffered mechanical issues, and Flinn heroically sacrificed the lives of himself and his men while avoiding civilian casualties. The B-26 crashed into an abandoned house in the tiny village of Rethondes, France, resulting in a great loss of life among the crew but none on the ground. While Flinn's body was buried in the Epinal American Cemetery in Epinal, France, a cenotaph (memorial marker) was placed outside the Flinn family mausoleum in Section 14 of The Homewood Cemetery to honor and memorialize him. (Courtesy of Hartwood Mansion.)

HENRY MILO CURRY.
BORN JANUARY 30. 1847.
DIED MAY 5. 1900.

HARRIET GIRTY CURRY.
BORN MARCH 12. 1850.
DIED FEBRUARY 7. 1914.

HENRY MILO CURRY (DIED 1900; SECTION 14). In 1863, with the Civil War raging all around him, 16-year-old Henry Milo Curry enlisted for duty as a private with the Union army. He mustered out as a sergeant several years later. Curry served with the Fifth Army Corps as a member of Company F, 155th Pennsylvania Volunteers. Although he engaged in several battles, he received only a minor wound at the Battle of Five Forks. Within a few days, he rejoined his unit, and he survived the war. (Courtesy of Becca Taylor.)

JAMES M. CURRY (DIED 1943; SECTION 14). A recipient of the honored Distinguished Service Cross, James M. Curry was also awarded the Silver Star for gallantry and the Purple Heart. Curry was killed in combat in Tunisia while serving with the 13th Armored Regiment during World War II. (Courtesy of Becca Taylor.)

Sgt. D. Edgar Maxwell and David Maxwell. Many parents promise to love and protect their children. Sometimes, that bond transcends death. When Sgt. D. Edgar Maxwell was killed on the battlefields of France during World War I, his father, David Maxwell, took issue with the length of time it was taking for France to return the bodies of those killed overseas. Along with many other Pittsburgh families who had lost soldiers, he founded the Bring Home the Soldier Dead League. The group successfully petitioned to have the remaining dead expeditiously repatriated to US soil, and there were soon chapters in many other cities throughout the country. In 1921, the body of Sgt. D. Edgar Maxwell was returned, and it now rests alongside his father, who fought so hard to bring him home. (Courtesy of the Library of Congress.)

UNIDENTIFIED WORLD WAR I VETERAN. It is difficult to comprehend the human toll of World War I, one of the deadliest conflicts in world history. Many who perished returned to the United States as "unknown soldiers." This picture from the cemetery archives shows the final resting place of just one of those soldiers. (Courtesy of The Homewood Cemetery.)

GEORGE COLLINSON BURGWIN JR. (DIED 1949; SECTION 11). After graduating from the University of Pittsburgh in 1917, George Collinson Burgwin Jr. served overseas as a captain in the Army with the 79th Infantry. He later became chancellor of the Episcopal Diocese of Pittsburgh—the third in a direct line and the fifth member of his family to occupy that role, which he held at the time of his death in 1949. (Courtesy of Elizabeth Burgwin.)

CAPT. JOHN WILKINS SR. (DIED 1809; SECTION 4). As the father of both Secretary of War William Wilkins and Gen. John Wilkins Jr., Capt. John Wilkins Sr. had a prosperous family that would leave its legacy in Pittsburgh. William later developed Homewood, the grounds which now contain the cemetery. When the cemetery was developed, Captain Wilkins's remains were transferred from their original resting place at Pittsburgh's Presbyterian Burying Ground and interred alongside the rest of the family in Section 4 at the Wilkins mausoleum. Capt. John Wilkins Sr. is believed to have the earliest date of birth of any individual buried at The Homewood Cemetery: 1733. (Courtesy of the Library of Congress.)

JAMES AND GLENNA GARNER (DIED 1960 AND 1918, RESPECTIVELY; SECTION 11). James Garner and his wife, Glenna, were essential in developing one of the foremost gas mask designs during World War I. Their design utilized activated charcoal to filter out the chlorine gas that was predominantly used at the time. The practicality of their invention was realized early in World War I, and their design was widely implemented, saving many lives. (Courtesy of the Library of Congress.)

FRANCIS FOWLER HOGAN, SOLDIER-POET (DIED 1918; SECTION 7). Francis Hogan was just 21 years old when he was killed in the cold, dark forest of the Argonne by machine-gun fire mere days before the end of World War I. But in those tender years, he had seen more than most. His friend Hervey Allen later called him a "Soldier-Poet" and dedicated an ode to Hogan's bravery. Hogan was a poet, and his piece "Fulfillment," written while fighting in France, was published alongside the works of George Orwell. Hogan wrote: "Think not my life has been futile / Nor grieve for an unsaid word / For all that my lips might never sing / My singing heart has heard." (Courtesy of the Library of Congress.)

JOHN WILKINS JR. (DIED 1816; SECTION 4). John Wilkins Jr. was the son of a captain of the American Revolution. Military achievement was in his nature, and it was no surprise when he enlisted to fight in the Revolution at the age of 15. He served as a surgeon's mate with the 4th Pennsylvania Regiment. In 1793, he was appointed to the position of brigadier general of the Allegheny County Militia to respond to the Whiskey Rebellion, which was overtaking the area. In 1796, he was chosen as quartermaster general of the US Army by Pres. George Washington. Upon his death in 1816, he was buried at the First Presbyterian Church. Later, when the family plot was designated at The Homewood Cemetery, he was reinterred alongside the rest of his family members. (Courtesy of The Homewood Cemetery.)

THE BURGWIN BOYS, OFF TO WAR. This striking image cannot be fully appreciated without understanding its context. On the eve of the First World War, these members of the Burgwin family— including fathers, sons, sons-in-law, and brothers— united for one family photograph before they went their separate ways in war. The photograph was taken to preserve that moment in time and their memories should they not survive. One man in each row wears a black armband over his uniform—Augustus P. Burgwin (first row, far right) and his son, Pierce Butler Carlisle Burgwin (second row, far left). They wore the armbands to honor Mildred Burgwin, wife of Augustus and mother of Pierce, who died shortly before this photograph was taken. (Courtesy of Elizabeth Burgwin.)

PIERCE BUTLER CARLISLE BURGWIN JR. (DIED 1994; SECTION 10). Following in the footsteps of a family steeped in military history, Pierce Butler Carlisle Burgwin Jr. enlisted in the US Army Air Corps during World War II. Outside of his military career, he had several children with his wife, Elizabeth Feeley Burgwin. They are both now at rest, along with several of their children, in the peaceful Burgwin family plot at The Homewood Cemetery. (Courtesy of Elizabeth Burgwin.)

JAMES MARTINUS SCHOONMAKER (DIED 1927; SECTION 14). Col. James Martinus Schoonmaker was awarded the Medal of Honor for his part in the Third Battle of Winchester on September 19, 1864, during the Civil War. His citation notes: "At a critical period, Colonel Schoonmaker gallantly led a cavalry charge against the left of the enemy's line of battle, drove the enemy out of his works, and captured many prisoners." After the war, Schoonmaker achieved success in the coke and banking industries in Pittsburgh. (Courtesy of the Library of Congress.)

Stewart McClintic (Died 1982; Section 14). As a civil engineer, Stewart McClintic's job came with a high degree of accountability. Assuming that role during wartime was an entirely different level of responsibility. While stationed in London as a lieutenant colonel, McClintic analyzed reports to specifically coordinate military bombing campaigns against the Nazis. He became known for his strategy and precision, both of which ultimately saved countless lives. He also worked on the Ultra project, which intercepted German communications sent via the Enigma cipher machine. These efforts earned him the Order of the British Empire and the French Croix de Guerre. In London, he met and married his wife, Pamela, (a war widow and Red Cross ambulance driver), and the couple had two children. McClintic's postwar career focused on the banking industry, which served him well as he reviewed the finances as a key figure in the Carnegie Hero Fund Commission, which he joined in 1947. (Courtesy of the Carnegie Hero Fund Commission.)

2ND LT. ELMER TAYLOR, TUSKEGEE AIRMAN (DIED 1944; SECTION 12). There are men who fight wars, and there are men who fight wars on two fronts. Elmer Taylor was one of the latter. Taylor was killed in action in an aircraft accident on June 2, 1944, while serving with Col. B.O. Davis and the 332nd Fighter Group of the Tuskegee Airmen at Ramitelli Airfield in Italy. Prior to his military career, Taylor attended Schenley High School and Virginia State College, where he was a member of the Omega Psi Pi fraternity. In 1943, he graduated from Tuskegee University's air school. This elite unit was comprised strictly of African American pilots who flew Bell P-39 Airacobras, Republic P-47 Thunderbolts, and North American P-51 Mustangs. The 332nd painted the tails of their planes red, earning them the nickname "Red Tails." Second Lieutenant Taylor's courage and sacrifice speak on behalf of the thousands of others who served alongside him, carrying on the lasting legacy of the Tuskegee Airmen. (Courtesy of the Collection of the Smithsonian National Museum of African American History and Culture.)

Donald C. Jefferson (Died 1994; Section 19). If one considered only the early part of Donald Jefferson's life, it would be easy to view him as a pioneer and a hero. Drafted in 1917, Jefferson was awarded with an officer's commission for his service. This was a noteworthy achievement and exceedingly rare for African Americans at the time. Jefferson served alongside other African American troops assigned to the 351st Field Artillery, shown here at the time of their return home on the deck of the *Louisville* in 1919. After the war, Jefferson continued to be a pioneer. His Lincoln Drug Company in East Liberty was noted as the first business owned by an African American in that area. He later served as a vice chairman of both the Allegheny County Housing Authority and the Allegheny County Redevelopment Authority Board of Directors. A few years before his death, he received a commendation from the Pennsylvania House of Representatives for his efforts toward achieving equality throughout his lifetime. (Courtesy of the National Archives and Records Administration.)

LIZETTE BEBOUT (DIED 1947; SECTION 13). As the heroes of World War I laid strewn across the battlefields of Europe, families in the United States struggled with the decisions surrounding repatriating the dead. To do so would mean an arduous journey across the sea to the land they once called home. Many families chose to leave their loved ones where they fell. These loved ones were commemorated in fields of honor such as the Meuse-Argonne American Cemetery in France. In all, over 46,000 soldiers were brought home to the United States for burial, while another 30,000 remained in Europe. Lt. James Dallas Bebout was one of those who remained with his fallen comrades. His mother, Lizette Bebout, accepted the government's offer to visit her son's grave in France. In 1930, years after the end of the First World War, she boarded the steamer *Republic* to visit her son, who would never again return home. (Courtesy of Becca Taylor.)

LUCY L. JOHNSON (DIED 1945; SECTION 26). Like the Gold Star Mothers shown here at the Tomb of the Unknown Soldier, Lucy L. Johnson lost a son. While her son Howard was serving in France, he was killed as the result of an electrical accident. He was buried in Thiaucourt, France, at St. Mihiel American Cemetery. Pittsburgh's local African American newspaper, the *Courier*, noted that she traveled with a pilgrimage of other Gold Star Mothers in July 1930. Upon her return from this visit, she attended many veteran events and served as a speaker at both memorial and political functions. She continued to provide a voice to preserve the patriotism that her son had fought and died for until her own death. (Courtesy of the Library of Congress.)

CAPT. DAVID E. BOWSER (DIED 1995; SECTION 21). *Semper fidelis*, the Marine Corps motto, means "Always Faithful." For David Bowser, it was a way of life. Assigned to Attack Squadron 251, Bowser was one of few to earn a fighter pilot designation. He served domestically and also in Bosnia and Italy. After safely landing a crippled F/A-18 strike fighter, he was awarded the Navy Achievement Medal in 1991. He applied for a regular commission but was killed in a training accident before finding out he'd received the honor. A chaplain shared the news with his family at his funeral. David is pictured here on his wedding day just a few short months before his accident. He was survived by his wife, Tracy; his beloved dog, Monty; his sisters, Amy and Holly; and his parents, Joanne and Dr. Ellsworth Bowser. Perhaps these words from his father describe him best: "David was highly motivated, and very dedicated. He was the making of a man, who wanted to be a Marine." With that dream achieved, his honor will forever remain. (Courtesy of the Bowser family.)

Four

DARING DAMES

Many of the women within this chapter were products of their times. They were born in eras that demanded civil and social conformity and placed little focus on the dreams or aspirations of women as individuals. Some were eternally memorialized on headstones with epithets that simply read "wife," as if their legacies held no value outside of that designation. By and large, women of earlier social eras were expected to marry well and have children, and their own value was strictly defined by such criteria. By those standards, many of the women included here did well. Their husbands were notable, and their aesthetically pleasing homes were blessed with many children. But outside of these familial achievements, they were destined for so much more. Helen Clay Frick left a rich legacy of philanthropy and art that benefits scholarly society to this day. Marie Ritz placed herself in war-torn Europe during World War I and bettered the lives of countless children by doing so. Daisy Lampkin was a force to be reckoned with and provided a voice for the African American community when they, like women, were part of a marginalized minority to whom few would listen. Brilliant minds like Bertha Lamme—a pioneering female electrical engineer—were trailblazers in their careers, which they were sadly expected to sacrifice upon marriage. Many in Pittsburgh will not only recognize the name of Elsie Hillman but have, without a doubt, benefited from both her philanthropy and her boundless perseverance as a woman who stood shoulder to shoulder with US presidents. Some of these women exemplified a quiet resolve, while others shouted from the rooftops. These are the women who persevered through adversity, fought against social norms, and defined their own meaning of greatness within their lifetimes. They represent only a small portion of the thousands of women buried within The Homewood Cemetery who led lives that are worthy of honoring and remembering. Some were contemporaries, some were separated by lifetimes, but all were daring dames.

37 UNION SQR. N.Y.

ADELAIDE HOWARD CHILDS FRICK (DIED 1931; SECTION 14). As the wife of Henry Clay Frick, Adelaide was one of the best-known society hostesses of her time. She is shown below in that capacity. Like many women of her era, she is often viewed through the lens of her husband's success. In letters to her surviving children (two died before the age of seven), a more intimate portrait arises of a woman who was a wife, a mother, and an individual in her own right. Her familial dedication is evident to this day in the details of Clayton, the home the family shared in Pittsburgh. (Left, courtesy of the Frick Collection/Frick Art Reference Library Archives; below, courtesy of the Library of Congress.)

Helen Clay Frick (Died 1984; Section 14). The third of Adelaide and Henry Clay Frick's four children, Helen was one of two who survived into adulthood. She inherited her father's love of art and worked diligently to preserve and document the family's legendary art collection. Helen established the Frick Art Reference Library in 1920. Her philanthropy extended to the University of Pittsburgh, where her funding helped build the famed Cathedral of Learning. Helen never married, and she died at the family home, Clayton. After her death, the home was converted into a museum that remains open to the public today. (Both, courtesy of the Frick Collection/ Frick Art Reference Library Archives.)

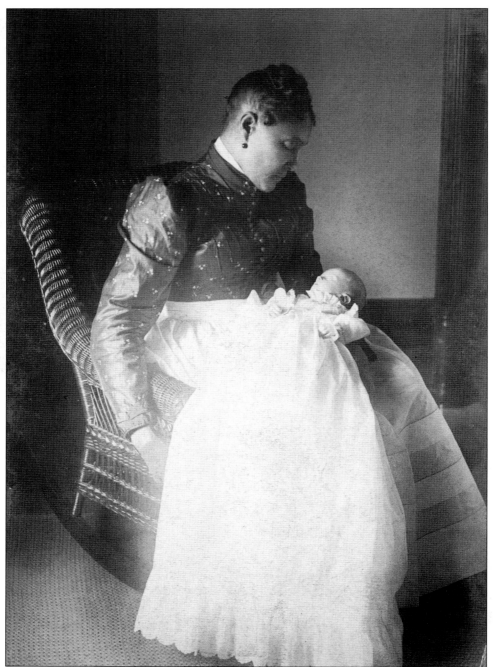

JANE GRANDISON (DIED 1896; SECTION 3). Jane Grandison left a great legacy of caring for others. As a nurse to the family of Henry Clay Frick, she cared for several of the Frick children, including Henry Clay Frick Jr., pictured here. Henry Jr., along with his sister Martha, did not survive to adulthood. After her time with the Frick children, Grandison and several friends established the Home for Aged and Infirm Colored Women, where she served as president. (Courtesy of the Frick Collection/Frick Art Reference Library Archives.)

LELA COCHRAN HILL BURGWIN (DIED 2002; SECTION 11). Pictured here at the time of her high school graduation, Lela Cochran Hill married George Collinson Burgwin III in 1949. Together, they raised a family while Lela focused her efforts on becoming a well-known real estate agent. Additionally, she volunteered for many organizations, among them Head Start, Episcopal Church Home, Shadyside Hospital, and the Anna B. Heldman Community Center (now Hill House). (Courtesy of Elizabeth Burgwin.)

ENID BOLI (DIED 1975; SECTION 7). Along with sixty-five nurses and one additional stenographer, typist Enid Boli was among the first group of women sent to provide assistance to troops fighting in Europe in August 1917. The University of Pittsburgh Base Hospital 27 was later assigned to Algiers. She survived the chaotic hell of war and returned to Pittsburgh, where she became the head librarian at the Wylie Avenue Carnegie Library in 1934. (Courtesy of the Library of Congress.)

ELSIE HILLIARD HILLMAN (DIED 2015; SECTION 25). Philanthropy, volunteering, and giving were important parts of Elsie Hillman's upbringing. Her mother instilled those values in her as a young child, and they would continue throughout Elsie's life. Serving as a Republican National Committee member, Elsie worked with prominent Republicans such as Dick Thornburg, Tom Ridge, Sen. John Heinz, and Pres. George Herbert Walker Bush. She also fostered bipartisan relationships with Democrats by focusing efforts on advancing causes such as civil and women's rights and promoting jobs throughout her native Pittsburgh. (Courtesy of the Hillman Foundation.)

MARIE RITZ (DIED 1952; SECTION 9).
Marie Ritz, the widow of Pittsburgh's
French consul, Louis Ritz, taught French
at Winchester Thurston for years after
her husband's death. When World War I
ravaged the countries of Europe, she put
her teaching job on hold and traveled
to France, Romania, Hungary, Bulgaria,
and Russia. Once back in the United
States, she continued raising money
for displaced families and children and
received the Reconnaissance Française
citation along with Le Secours de
Guerre, a relief agency for war victims.
(Courtesy of the Library of Congress.)

**ETHEL DWYER MCCRADY (DIED
1985; COLUMBARIUM).** Born in
Tarrytown, New York, on the eve
of the 20th century, Ethel Dwyer
pursued the life of a chorus girl
that beckoned so many of the era,
starring in movies such as *Ten Nights
in a Bar Room* and a stage production
of *Tarzan*. She later landed the
lead role in *Abbie's Irish Rose*. She
married Roland McCrady in 1924
and retired from acting, going on
to have two children. (Courtesy
of the Library of Congress.)

MARY FRANK KIMBALL (DIED 1911; SECTION 9). In 1888, Mary was born to Frank and Keren Kimball in Beloit, Ohio. The family later moved to Pittsburgh. In her relatively short lifetime, Mary achieved a rare accomplishment for women of the era—she attended college. After her graduation from Smith College in Northampton, Massachusetts, Mary returned to her family home in Pittsburgh. Sadly, she died at that home in 1911 at the young age of 23, with her obituary in the *Pittsburgh Daily Post* noting that "hard study, it is believed, undermined her health." (Courtesy of The Homewood Cemetery.)

LOUISA JEANNETTE EDWARDS (DIED 1902; SECTION 14). After graduating with honors from Thurston Preparatory School, Louisa (daughter of Ogden and Sarah Herron Edwards) pursued college at the prestigious Ogontz School for Young Ladies, where she was president of her class. Upon graduation, she returned to the social circles of her hometown of Pittsburgh. Shortly thereafter, she was stricken with a devastating bout of pneumonia. She died suddenly of a weakened heart while visiting Atlantic City in 1902. (Courtesy of the Library of Congress.)

GEORGE M. DALLAS.
Vice President of the United States

MATILDA DALLAS WILKINS (DIED 1881; SECTION 4). One of several children born to a prominent Philadelphia family in 1798, Matilda Dallas was surrounded by political circles throughout her life. Her brother George Mifflin Dallas (pictured) held prominence in his hometown and, eventually, the entire country. In 1828, he was elected mayor of Philadelphia. His political career led to him serving as the 11th vice president of the United States from 1845 to 1849. As her brother's political star rose, Matilda Dallas married Judge William Wilkins. William and Matilda's mansion, Homewood, is the namesake for the cemetery in which they are both now buried. (Courtesy of the Library of Congress.)

THE GYPSY FORTUNE TELLER

COUNTESS MINNIE BLANCA DE OVIES (DIED 1927; SECTION 14). Although she was a countess due to her marriage to an exiled Spanish count, Minnie Blanca de Ovies had humble roots. She was born Minnie Blanche McDonald in Coshocton, Ohio, in 1860. After marrying, Countess Blanca moved in elite social circles, mesmerizing them with great feats of palm-reading and fortune telling. With her husband, she spent time pursuing these endeavors at the Lily Dale spiritualist community in New York. Upon the death of her husband, she advanced her career by exploring early facets of criminal psychology. After she died from heart failure in 1927, she was buried in the family plot of her dear friend Lillian Pitcairn Taylor. (Courtesy of the Library of Congress.)

RUTH TOWNLEY (DIED 1976; SECTION 12). The tombstone of Ruth Townley is decorated with the Women's Overseas Service League insignia. It serves as a small reminder of her great volumes of humanitarian work. Beginning in November 1918, she was stationed at Bourges, France, as an employee of—and later director of—the canteen. In this vital role, she provided sustenance for soldiers and the community in addition to serving in an informative capacity for one of the main ports for soldiers returning home. She herself would not make that return journey until October 1919. Following the war, she maintained an alliance with the groups she supported in France in addition to becoming a teacher at Schenley High School. (Courtesy of the Library of Congress.)

PAMELA GRESSON MCCLINTIC (DIED 1982; SECTION 14). Surreal scenes such as the one shown here became commonplace during the Nazi bombing raids of London in World War II. In the midst of tragedy, however, there were shining examples of courageous selflessness, such as Pamela Gresson McClintic. Pamela served with the Red Cross as an ambulance driver. While most were trying to escape scenes like this, her role demanded direct involvement. As a war widow, she understood the magnitude of the losses so many suffered. She later found happiness with an American military intelligence agent (Stewart McClintic), and after the war, they lived in the United States with their two children. It is a credit to her courage and sacrifice that other families and children survived the war as well. (Courtesy of the Library of Congress.)

4377-4

CHRISTINE MILLER CLEMSON (DIED 1956; SECTION 14). Christine Miller was a girl with a golden voice—so much so that an anonymous benefactor paid for her musical education. Her talents took her far, and she was soon one of the top contraltos, performing at theaters and palaces across the world. At the peak of her popularity, she returned home, accepting a job as a soloist for the Third Presbyterian Church. There, she met and married wealthy older parishioner Daniel Clemson, only to find out that he was the anonymous benefactor who launched her career. After Daniel's death, Christine joined starlet Lillian Russell in raising their voices in unison to sell war bonds on the streets of downtown Pittsburgh. She left a quiet philanthropic legacy that is fondly remembered to this day. (Courtesy of the Library of Congress.)

TIME
THE WEEKLY NEWSMAGAZINE

Boris Chaliapin

WASHINGTON HOSTESS PERLE MESTA
The right men come to dinner.

PERLE MESTA (DIED 1975; SECTION 21). Known as the "Hostess with the Mostess," Perle Mesta thrived in elaborate social and political circles throughout her life. Upon the death of her husband, manufacturing giant George Mesta, she inherited his fortune. She eventually moved to Washington, DC, where she rubbed elbows with the high-powered elite, including many political aficionados. Perle staunchly supported the Equal Rights Amendment and the National Women's Party and later became involved with the Democratic Party. Harry S. Truman appointed her as ambassador to Luxembourg. During Truman's presidency, Perle was known for throwing lavish soirées that included senators, congressmen, and high-ranking political appointees on the guest lists. In March 1949, Perle was featured on the cover of *Time* magazine, which lauded her for her numerous social and political contributions to society. (Courtesy of The Homewood Cemetery.)

AGNES TAYLOR (DIED 1957; SECTION 14). To say the 1950s were a difficult time for African Americans is an understatement. Many were turned away from things as basic as lodging solely because of the color of their skin. Agnes Taylor, an African American and former nurse, sought to change that. Together with her sister, she opened the Agnes Taylor Tourist Home, an establishment similar to the one pictured here. Her hotel was listed in *The Negro Motorist Green-Book*, a guide that assisted people of color in finding establishments where they would be welcomed while traveling. Her clientele included everyone from general travelers to celebrities such as Nat King Cole. Taylor is now at rest in a grave in Section 14—she is the only African American woman known to be buried in that section. (Courtesy of the Library of Congress.)

"THE PRINCESS" DORIS MERCER (DIED 1963; SECTION 9). Doris Mercer, the daughter of a Pittsburgh police officer, joined the ranks of chorus girls on the stages of New York City at age 18. Her first marriage, to publisher Percival Harden, ended in 1919. In 1924, she married Sebastian Kresge, the multimillionaire founder of a chain of stores. Their marriage lasted only a few years, and they divorced in 1928. Leaving the United States behind, she traveled to Paris and lived alongside the aristocracy. She was courted by a member of Persian royalty, Prince Farid Khan Sadri-Kajar, and they married in 1933. Although they eventually divorced, and she moved back to the United States, Princess Farid-es-Sultaneh refused to give up her title. She lived her remaining years at her estate in New Jersey and was known simply as the Princess until her death. (Both, courtesy of The Homewood Cemetery.)

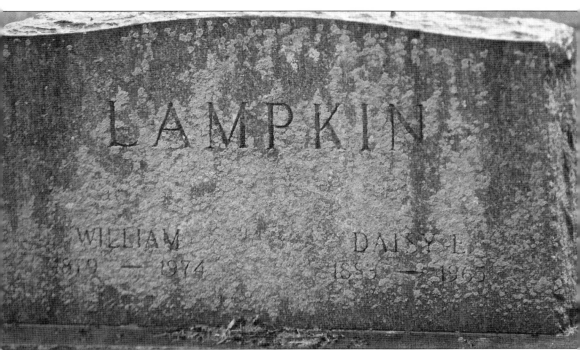

Daisy Lampkin (Died 1965; Section 12). Daisy Lampkin was a force to be reckoned with. She is best known for her work with the civil rights movement but was also devoted to the suffragette movement. Lampkin helped develop branches of the NAACP and the Urban League in Pittsburgh. She served as vice president of the *Courier* and used that platform to give a much-needed voice to issues affecting the African American population. Focusing her efforts in her hometown of Pittsburgh and also on a national level, she served as the national field secretary for the NAACP. In 1938, she recognized the potential and promise of a young attorney and nurtured his involvement with the NAACP's Legal Defense Committee. His name was Thurgood Marshall, and he later won *Brown v. Board of Education of Topeka* and went on to become a Supreme Court justice. (Courtesy of Becca Taylor.)

Bertha Lamme Feicht (Died 1943; Section 24). At a time when most women didn't have a voice, Bertha Lamme wrote a thesis called "An Analysis of Tests of a Westinghouse Railway Generator." This earned her a mechanical engineering degree from Ohio State University (the university's library is pictured here). Her brother Benjamin was an engineer at Westinghouse, and he brought Bertha's work to the attention of Supt. Albert Schmid, who was so impressed with her capabilities that he hired her as an electrical engineer. She helped advance technology at a time when Westinghouse was critical to developing electricity as a power source throughout the country and the world. When she married in 1905, she gave up her career (as was customary) in order to maintain the family's household. However, her short 12-year career was not forgotten, and she left a lasting legacy, having served as the first female electrical engineer in the United States. (Courtesy of the Library of Congress.)

JILL VICTORIA WATSON (DIED 1996; SECTION 20). After graduating from Carnegie Mellon University in 1987, Jill Watson became a partner with the architectural firm of Arthur Lubetz Associates. She received numerous awards for her work and served as adjunct professor of architecture at Carnegie Mellon. Her invaluable legacy is honored at the Jill Watson Festival Across the Arts and by many who stop to appreciate the famed Pittsburgh mural *The Bride of Penn Avenue*, Watson's collaboration with muralist Judy Penzer. Laura Nettleton, Watson's former teacher and a family friend, worked with Watson's parents to design a monument for Jill after she was killed in the crash of TWA Flight 800. At noon on January 20, Jill Watson's birthday, sunlight streams through the center of the semicircular monument, illuminating the inscription, which reads, in part: "We knew the real meaning of grief when we no longer could see your bright face. We will never forget you." (Courtesy of Becca Taylor.)

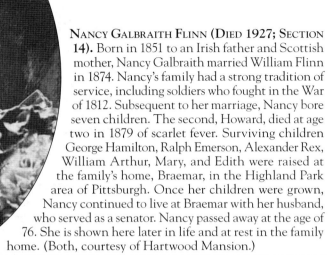

NANCY GALBRAITH FLINN (DIED 1927; SECTION 14). Born in 1851 to an Irish father and Scottish mother, Nancy Galbraith married William Flinn in 1874. Nancy's family had a strong tradition of service, including soldiers who fought in the War of 1812. Subsequent to her marriage, Nancy bore seven children. The second, Howard, died at age two in 1879 of scarlet fever. Surviving children George Hamilton, Ralph Emerson, Alexander Rex, William Arthur, Mary, and Edith were raised at the family's home, Braemar, in the Highland Park area of Pittsburgh. Once her children were grown, Nancy continued to live at Braemar with her husband, who served as a senator. Nancy passed away at the age of 76. She is shown here later in life and at rest in the family home. (Both, courtesy of Hartwood Mansion.)

MARY FLINN LAWRENCE (DIED 1974; SECTION 14). Brilliant, educated, and charming, Mary Flinn Lawrence attended the Thurston School in Pittsburgh, followed by Briarcliff College in New York, from which she graduated in 1906. She became involved in charity work through her father's affiliation with the Industrial Home for Crippled Children. The experience deeply affected her, and it remained a cause close to her heart. Young Mary saw many opportunities for change, and in 1912, she became president of the Allegheny County Equal Franchise Federation, a suffragist organization dedicated to helping women secure the right to vote. When World War I erupted, Lawrence helped organize the Suffrage Red Cross, which focused on the war effort. A staunch Republican, Lawrence maintained a close friendship with Teddy Roosevelt, and the two often exchanged personal correspondence. Outside of politics, Lawrence was well known in the equestrian arena. She built Hartwood Acres Estate, where she lived with her husband, John, and their two children. The 629-acre grounds, including the stately mansion, are now open for public enjoyment thanks to Mary Lawrence's unending generosity. (Both, courtesy of Hartwood Mansion.)

EDITH GALBRAITH FLINN PATTERSON (DIED 1961; SECTION 14). Like her sister Mary, Edith was raised to be an educated woman. After college, she raised a family with her husband, Simon Truby Patterson. Edith had a lifelong passion for horses and competed in equestrian events throughout her lifetime. This was a skill her children shared. Their residence, Harkaway Farms, was located on the present grounds of Hartwood Acres Estate. Their home often served as a place of respite for soldiers, for whom Edith would provide home-cooked meals as they passed through Pittsburgh on the way to destinations unknown. (Both, courtesy of Hartwood Mansion.)

RUTH EDWARDS WELLS (DIED 1936; SECTION 14). Ruth Edwards was the fourth and last child of Mr. and Mrs. Ogden M. Edwards. After completing her education, she married Pittsburgh businessman Albert Wells in Shady Side Presbyterian Church (pictured). Her uncle, Rev. Maurice D. Edwards, DD, officiated their ceremony in front of many friends and family. (Courtesy of the Library of Congress.)

MARGARET BLAIR BURGWIN (DIED 2011; SECTION 10). Pictured here on the day of her wedding to Lane Carpenter, Margaret Blair Burgwin was the daughter of Pierce Butler Carlisle Burgwin Jr. and Elizabeth Feeley Burgwin. She dedicated her life to helping mothers and children through her career as an ultrasonographer in the town of State College, Pennsylvania. (Courtesy of Elizabeth Burgwin.)

CLARA LOUISE NEGLEY FLINN (DIED 1966; SECTION 4). In 1900, six years before this photograph of Shadyside Presbyterian Church was taken, Clara Louise Negley married George Hamilton Flinn with light streaming through the luminous rose window. In its coverage of the social event, the April 27, 1900, *Pittsburgh Daily Post* noted, "Miss Negley, always a pretty girl, made a lovely bride in her wedding gown of cream-tinted satin with full court train, and her neck and arms, softly pink, shining through the meshes of rose pointe which composed the yoke and sleeves of her bodice. Descending from her bouquet of lilies of the valley were innumerable strands of narrow white satin ribbon entwined and tipped with little white clusters of flowers. Her veil of tulle fell from a small coronet of orange blossoms, and not the smallest jewel was worn." Their marriage lasted for nearly three decades until George's death in 1929. (Courtesy of the Library of Congress.)

Five

TALENT AND TENACITY

One does not have to reside in Pittsburgh to respect its reputation as a sports town. Like an old, worn baseball card placed between the pages of a book, the stories of notable Pittsburghers such as Pie Traynor and Jock Sutherland are part of the city's history. Pittsburgh also has a rich legacy of musical and artistic talent, with figures such as Walt Harper and Erroll Garner gracing its storied stages. In varying ways, and in different eras, artists like George Hetzel and Teenie Harris captured the essence of the community and its landscapes. All of these respected individuals, through their gifted abilities, speak to moments in time when urbanization, social development, and civil rights were at the forefront. While the sports stars within this chapter certainly left impressive records, the artistic talents of others captured daily lives that were punctuated with the vocal and literary gifts of several notable Pittsburghers. Such talent does not exist in a vacuum. It requires dedication and commitment, whether it be musical, athletic, artistic, or literary. The individuals within this chapter are known and remembered for their creative and skilled contribution to society. They are artists and entertainers, and their legacies are presented here long after they were first recognized for their talent and tenacity.

CHARLES "TEENIE" HARRIS (DIED 1998; SECTION 12). Through this very camera (now housed in the Smithsonian), *Pittsburgh Courier* photographer Teenie Harris captured not only images of celebrities like Muhammad Ali and John F. Kennedy but also the minutiae of everyday life in his Hill District community. He encapsulated the early 20th century, when Pittsburgh's African American population was experiencing oppression and opulence. Though oppressed, the Hill District reached the heights of jazz culture, featuring greats like Erroll Garner, Earl "Fatha" Hines, Count Basie, Duke Ellington, Billy Strayhorn, Thelonious Monk, Walt Harper, Ethel Fields, Dizzy Gillespie, Ella Fitzgerald, and Etta James, to name a few. Teenie photographed them all. His images also represented the community, providing a visual legacy of children at school, sporting events, funerals, weddings, and family gatherings. His collection of over 80,000 images tells stories both famous and unknown, forever cherished and remembered. (Courtesy of the collection of the Smithsonian National Museum of African American History and Culture, gift from Charles A. Harris and Beatrice Harris in memory of Charles "Teenie" Harris.)

RALPH "LEFTY" MELLIX (DIED 1985; SECTION 33). The Pittsburgh Crawfords and the Homestead Grays were legendary Negro League baseball teams, and Lefty Mellix was legendary on both. Mellix played alongside other greats such as Josh Gibson and Satchel Paige. Throughout his 35-year career, he played in 1,500 games, including nine no-hitters. (Courtesy of the Library of Congress.)

JOHN KINLEY TENER (DIED 1946; SECTION 12). John Kinley Tener knew how to play hardball. At a towering six feet and four inches, he played professional baseball as a pitcher and an outfielder for teams such as the Chicago White Stockings and the Pittsburgh Burghers. After retiring from baseball, Tener pursued a career in politics, winning a seat in the 61st US Congress in Pennsylvania's 24th Congressional District. He served as governor of Pennsylvania from 1911 to 1915. For a short time, he also served as the president of baseball's National League. (Courtesy of the Library of Congress.)

CHARLES H. COOPER (DIED 1984; SECTION 32). Chuck Cooper was already a basketball legend when he graduated from Westinghouse High School in 1944. He went on to play for Duquesne University and the Harlem Globetrotters. In 1950, he became one of the first African Americans drafted by the NBA and began playing for the Boston Celtics. He was once and always a Pittsburgh son and held several positions with the city after his basketball career. (Courtesy of The Homewood Cemetery.)

HAROLD "PIE" TRAYNOR (DIED 1972; SECTION 20). Pie Traynor spent most of his life as a memorable figure in Pittsburgh baseball history. His entire career as a third baseman, from 1920 to 1937, was spent with the Pittsburgh Pirates. In 1948, he became the first third baseman inducted into the Baseball Hall of Fame. Traynor then spent an additional 21 years working as a sports radio broadcaster. (Courtesy of the Library of Congress.)

JOHN BAIN "JOCK" SUTHERLAND (DIED 1948; SECTION 24). Jock Sutherland was a standout football player under renowned coach Pop Warner at the University of Pittsburgh. He was an All-American and played on the 1915 and 1916 championship teams in addition to being part of the undefeated 1917 team. In 1924, Sutherland replaced Warner as head coach of Pitt's football team. His record of 111–20–12 speaks for itself. After his coaching career, Sutherland served his country in the US Navy as a lieutenant commander during World War II. After the war, he proudly served as head coach for the Pittsburgh Steelers and led the team to its first playoffs in 1947. (Courtesy of the Archives Service Center, University of Pittsburgh.)

GEORGE HETZEL (DIED 1899; SECTION 7). George Hetzel got his start painting riverboat rooms and local saloons. In the mid-19th century, his style evolved, and he became the founder of the Scalp Level school of painting. His reputation continued to grow, and he was included in the 1876 Centennial Exposition, the 1893 Columbian Exposition, and the 1896 Carnegie International. A landscape painted by Hetzel was the first documented art purchase made by legendary collector Henry Clay Frick and still hangs in Clayton (the Frick family home) today. (Courtesy of Frick Art & Historical Center, Pittsburgh.)

THE FRIEBERTSHAUSER DAUGHTERS (SECTIONS 5 AND 8). At the turn of the 20th century, Pittsburgh was known as an industrial capital. Around that same time, great achievements were being made in the arts and music. William Friebertshauser, a timpanist, was one of the original members of the Pittsburgh Orchestra (now the Pittsburgh Symphony Orchestra). The rest of the family was likewise musically gifted. One of William's eight daughters, Adala, was a well-reputed soprano. She is pictured with her sisters, Helen, Alma, Celenia, Selma, Laura, Cora, and Emma. (Courtesy of The Homewood Cemetery.)

ERROLL GARNER (DIED 1977; SECTION 12). Erroll Garner could not read music, but he sure could play it. By the age of 11, he was sneaking out of the house to play on riverboats in his hometown of Pittsburgh. He moved to New York City in 1944 and played with greats like Charlie Parker, and he appeared many times on *The Tonight Show Starring Johnny Carson*. His best known composition, "Misty," became a hallmark of Johnny Mathis and was covered by Sarah Vaughan, Ella Fitzgerald, Frank Sinatra, and Aretha Franklin, among others. (Courtesy of Erroll Garner Archive, 1942–2010, AIS.2015.09, Archives & Special Collections, University of Pittsburgh Library System.)

WALT HARPER (DIED 2006; SECTION 12). Walt Harper was born and raised in a musical family during the golden age of the Pittsburgh jazz scene. After attending Schenley High School, he focused on musical studies for several years before pursuing his career as a jazz pianist. After studying at the sides of greats like Erroll Garner, he was well prepared. Harper's band became a staple at the Hill District's famed Crawford Grill jazz club throughout the 1960s, and Harper eventually opened his own clubs in downtown Pittsburgh that featured jazz greats such as Cannonball Adderley, Mel Tormé, and Wynton Marsalis, among others. (Courtesy of the Library of Congress.)

SIMON TRUBY PATTERSON (DIED 1937; SECTION 14). While attending Yale during the first decade of the 20th century, Simon Truby Patterson became well-known in its literary circles. His short story "The Seventh" appeared in volume 43 of the *Yale Courant*, which was published in November 1906. The following year, the *Yale Literary Magazine* noted that Patterson was elected as book reviewer for the *Courant*. Alongside him in that class was a relatively unknown writer who would later become a household name—American novelist and playwright Sinclair Lewis. (Courtesy of the Library of Congress.)

Richard Rowland (Died 1947; Section 9). In 1915, studio executive and producer Richard Rowland started the Metro Pictures Corporation along with Louis B. Mayer. Several years later, Metro Pictures Corporation was sold to another film studio, and Rowland went to work with the Fox Film Corporation. The original Metro Pictures Corporation later merged with the Goldwyn Pictures Corporation, becoming what is now MGM (Metro-Goldwyn-Mayer) Studios. Rowland's legacy is commemorated with a star on the Hollywood Walk of Fame. (Courtesy of the Library of Congress.)

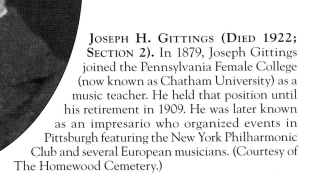

Joseph H. Gittings (Died 1922; Section 2). In 1879, Joseph Gittings joined the Pennsylvania Female College (now known as Chatham University) as a music teacher. He held that position until his retirement in 1909. He was later known as an impresario who organized events in Pittsburgh featuring the New York Philharmonic Club and several European musicians. (Courtesy of The Homewood Cemetery.)

MOTHERLESS. Renowned sculptor George Anderson Lawson studied in Rome and trained at the Royal Scottish Academy. His pieces have been displayed in famous locations across Europe. He depicted subjects such as the Duke of Wellington and Scottish poet Robert Burns. Just outside the Mellon mausoleum in The Homewood Cemetery sits another one of Lawson's creations, *Motherless.* The statue, which is both subtle and dramatic, is a bronze copy of the original, which resides in a Glasgow museum. This statue was kept in the gardens of James Ross Mellon (for whom the mausoleum was built). After his death, it was moved from the family home to his mausoleum, where it is now enjoyed and appreciated by countless visitors to the cemetery. (Courtesy of Becca Taylor.)

Six

HUMBLED HEARTS AND
STORIED SOULS

This chapter features names that readers might not know. Many were not recognized during their lifetimes; others never had much of a chance to live at all. They were inventors and pioneers, mothers and fathers and doctors, heroes and victims, and children who never had the chance to realize their full potential. Each has a tale to tell. Within this chapter are people ranging from Rust Heinz (a scion of the famous Heinz family) to community physicians like Dr. Robert Woods. This chapter also presents the stories of pioneers like Charles Beltz, the first to ride a newfangled machine called a bicycle through the streets of Pittsburgh. Treasured family members such as Hill Burgwin and Susan Patterson are fondly remembered. Victims and heroes of long-forgotten disasters such as an 1880 train derailment, the Harwick mine disaster of 1904, and the Equitable gas tank explosion of 1927 are honored in succinct anecdotes that can only hope to embrace a tiny portion of their legacies. Some of the smallest stories are from those who had the tiniest voices, and their unrecognized narratives are now memorialized. Albert Harper Dilworth and little Ida Spittle represent the countless children who have been lost to accidents, illness, and disease. They may not have changed the courses of nations, but their names and lives are worthy of remembrance.

37 UNION SQR, N.Y.

FRANK S. CURTO (DIED 1971; QUIET REFLECTIONS MAUSOLEUM). After graduating from Ohio State University with a degree in ornamental horticulture, Frank Curto was hired as the official horticulturist for the city of Pittsburgh in 1946. He later worked for the famed Phipps Conservatory, where he directed the well-known Fall Flower Show for more than two decades. His legacy continues with the many gardens cultivated within the park that now bears his name and overlooks the city he helped beautify. (Courtesy of the Library of Congress.)

MARTHA HOWARD FRICK (DIED 1891; SECTION 14). The second of the four Frick children, Martha was affectionately known by her father, Henry, as "Rosebud." As a young girl, Martha ingested a pin, causing an infection that resulted in her death just before she turned six. Martha's loss had a profound impact on the family. It is said that her father was holding her hand when she died and that he had the trees cleared so her grave at The Homewood Cemetery would remain visible from the nearby family home, Clayton. (Courtesy of the Frick Collection/Frick Art Reference Library Archives.)

RUST HEINZ AND THE PHANTOM CORSAIR (DIED 1939; SECTION 14). Grandson of the famous H.J. Heinz, Rust Heinz embodied the modernistic vision of the early 20th century. In 1938, a keen eye for design led him to develop this stylistically visionary prototype, known as the Phantom Corsair. It would be the only one ever produced. Tragically, Rust Heinz was killed in a car accident the following year, and the vehicle never went into production. (Courtesy of The Homewood Cemetery.)

DR. ROBERT ANDREW WOODS (DIED 1953; SECTION 14). This 1936 photograph shows Dr. Robert Woods standing at the foot of his own headstone, which he designed prior to his death. The doctor wrote his own epitaph, a biography of his life consisting of 1,005 letters. His late wife, Grace Lydia Street Woods, had written her own epitaph for the same stone prior to her death in 1935. (Courtesy of The Homewood Cemetery.)

HARWICK Mine Disaster
Jan 25 1904

THE CARNEGIE HERO FUND. The Carnegie Hero Fund, established in 1904 to recognize acts of selfless heroism, was inspired by Selwyn Taylor and Daniel Lyle, who lost their lives saving others from the Harwick mine disaster. The organization is now worldwide. In addition to Taylor and Louis A. Baumann Jr. (the first recipient of the Carnegie Hero Award), four Carnegie Hero Fund presidents—Charles L. Taylor, Thomas Shaw Arbuthnot, Charles Arbuthnot McClintock, and Stewart L. McClintic—are buried in The Homewood Cemetery. (Courtesy of the Library of Congress.)

THE EYMANS AND THE CARNEGIE HERO FUND. In 1932, Albert Eyman was at the beach when he saw a woman struggling against the current. Selflessly, he assisted in saving her life, but he died as a result of his effort. For this act, he was awarded the Carnegie Hero Award. One of his sons, Albert Jr. (pictured at left), received scholarship assistance from the commission. Another son, Herb, later became an esteemed investigator for the Carnegie Hero Fund. Both Albert Sr. and Herb now rest at The Homewood Cemetery. (Courtesy of the Carnegie Hero Fund Commission.)

CHARLES REED HARDY (DIED 1927; SECTION 19). It is an injustice to attempt to use words to encapsulate the scope of the event that rocked the North Side of Pittsburgh on November 14, 1927, at 8:43 a.m., when the Equitable gas tank—the largest gasometer in the world—exploded. The five-million-cubic-foot tank had developed a leak, and workers were sent to repair it with acetylene torches. The tank ignited, lifting it hundreds of feet into the air and causing the subsequent explosion of two neighboring tanks. Thousands of windows were shattered as far as miles away, and 26 people ultimately perished. Among them was Charles Reed Hardy, whose skull was fractured as a result of the explosion. (Courtesy of the Library of Congress.)

HOMER KEPPEL AND THE SADDEST SUNDAY (DIED 1880; SECTION 7). Newspaper accounts called it the "Saddest Sunday." On October 10, 1880, a train with several hundred passengers waited on the tracks near Pittsburgh's present-day Strip District while more people piled in following a parade. Unbeknownst to them, another train on the same line was barreling toward them in the darkness. The two collided, with the latter slamming into the former with enough force to upend the train car and shear off the steam valve. Death was massive and immediate, both from the concussion of the accident and the resulting steam explosion. Among the dead was Homer Keppel. Of the 26 people who died, 10 were buried at The Homewood Cemetery (including Keppel). (Courtesy of the Library of Congress.)

GETTING ON BROADWAY CAR

ALBERT HARPER DILWORTH (DIED 1893; SECTION 4). Like most 13-year-olds, Albert Harper Dilworth enjoyed a good football game. Unfortunately, he fell victim to a tragic accident after leaving such a game in 1893. With automobiles not yet common, young Albert followed what most people in that era did for transportation—he took a streetcar. While attempting to catch the streetcar after the game, he slipped beneath the wheels and was gravely injured. He was first taken to a nearby drugstore, where several doctors (including Dr. C.F. Bingaman) attempted to save both his leg and his life. They were unsuccessful, and he died shortly after being moved to his family's nearby house on Fifth Avenue. He had been his parents' only son. (Courtesy of the Library of Congress.)

"A BUD" 4.
Copyright 1901 by Otto Sarony

HOWARD NESBIT (DIED 1928; SECTION 23). As children at the start of the 20th century, Howard and his sister Florence Evelyn (pictured) grew up in abject poverty in a town called Tarentum outside of Pittsburgh. After the death of Howard and Florence's father, the family moved from Pittsburgh to Philadelphia and, ultimately, New York. Young Howard was often shuffled off to friends and relatives as his mother dedicated her focus to ensuring her daughter's social success. Howard's sister's name would eventually become much more recognizable than his—Evelyn Nesbit became the face of countless print advertising campaigns as the original Gibson Girl. Howard married and pursued a career as a salesman in New York. Years later, Evelyn married Harry Kendall Thaw of Pittsburgh. In 1906, Thaw shot architect Stanford White atop Madison Square Garden in New York in a dispute over Evelyn, resulting in the first trial described as the "Trial of the Century." (Courtesy of the Library of Congress.)

SUSAN LEE PATTERSON (DIED 2016; SECTION 10). Although they were not related by blood, Susan Patterson had always been a part of the household of Pierce Butler Carlisle Burgwin Jr. and Elizabeth Feeley Burgwin. As a teenager, Susan was a dear friend of the Burgwin children. Her place was made official when she was legally adopted by the Burgwins, and she remained a part of the family until her death. (Courtesy of Elizabeth Burgwin.)

GEORGE REESE PATTERSON (DIED 1973; SECTION 14). George was the beloved son of Edith Flinn and Simon Truby Patterson. His final resting place, within William Flinn's mausoleum, is marked with a simple but elegant plaque commemorating the day he arrived in this world and the day he left it. Beneath the inscription, the plaque is marked with a small two-word French phrase, *Chez soi*—which translates to "at home." (Courtesy of Becca Taylor.)

CHARLES BELTZ (DIED 1938; SECTION 2). In 1878, Charles Beltz became the first person to ride the a bicycle through the streets of Pittsburgh. By 1879, he had become a charter member of the Keystone Bicycle Club. For more than 50 years, bicycles were his business. He continued to ride until late in life, likely spending at least some of his early years on a bicycle like the one pictured here. (Courtesy of the Library of Congress.)

HILL BURGWIN (DIED 1946; SECTION 11). As the Civil War raged, the Burgwin family home in North Carolina was looted and burned. Silver heirlooms that had been in the family for generations were taken, sold, and/or lost. Over half a century later, Hill Burgwin dedicated himself to tracking down those items. He successfully recovered much of them from places as far away as antique shops in London, and in doing so, he restored many pieces of the family's legacy. (Courtesy of Elizabeth Burgwin.)

THE FLOWER-STREWN GRAVE.

LITTLE IDA SPITTLE (DIED 1898; SECTION 15). A little over four months old at the time of her death, Ida Spittle was buried in a lone grave. Researchers determined that she was the daughter of immigrants and had siblings—including, notably, a twin. Ida's small grave speaks to a bygone era of frequent infant mortality and is now sweetly tended by volunteers who still hold her close at heart. (Courtesy of the Library of Congress.)

Discover Thousands of Local History Books
Featuring Millions of Vintage Images

Arcadia Publishing, the leading local history publisher in the United States, is committed to making history accessible and meaningful through publishing books that celebrate and preserve the heritage of America's people and places.

Find more books like this at
www.arcadiapublishing.com

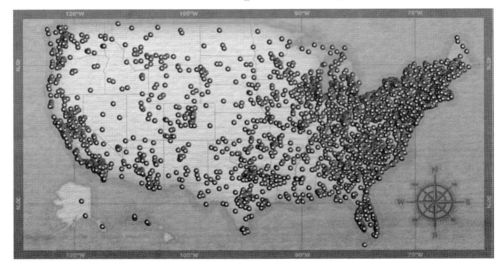

Search for your hometown history, your old stomping grounds, and even your favorite sports team.